A Special Gift

To _____

From _____

The
Father
Who
Calls

The Father Who Calls

Janette Oke

BETHANY HOUSE PUBLISHERS
MINNEAPOLIS, MINNESOTA 55438
A Division of Bethany Fellowship, Inc.

Editorial development by Blue Water Ink, Grand Rapids, Michigan.
Artwork by Roselyn B. Danner.

Copyright © 1988
All Rights Reserved

Published by Bethany House Publishers
A Division of Bethany Fellowship, Inc.
6820 Auto Club Road, Minneapolis, Minnesota 55438

Printed in the United States of America

Library of Congress Cataloging-in-Publication Data

Oke, Janette, 1935–
     The father who calls.
     (Canadian West series ;   )
     1. Meditations.   I. Title.   II. Series: Oke, Janette, 1935–   .
Canadian West series ;   .
BV4832.2.042   1988   242   88–22128
ISBN 1-55661-042-2   CIP

FOREWORD

We began the Canadian West series with a young, prosperous Easterner content with life but with an inner tug that called for stretching her wings and her faith. Elizabeth Thatcher answered that call by agreeing to travel west to brother Jon's country to teach in a needy area of the Alberta frontier.

To Elizabeth, born and bred to culture and refinement, the new venture held many challenges and learning experiences. One, she had not counted on. She met Wynn, a dashing, honor-bound and dedicated member of what is now the Royal Canadian Mounted Police. Elizabeth had vowed not to marry a Westerner—but we all have heard those kinds of statements before.

As we travel with Wynn and Elizabeth to their primitive postings to the harsh northern Indian villages, Elizabeth is forced to grow and change and become more than a pretty picture in the latest fashionable gown. She met the challenge and became a wife and helpmate in every sense of the word.

The hardest burden for Elizabeth to carry was her barrenness. Women readers have understood and shared her pain. Our children are so dear, and to be denied the experience of motherhood seems too great a sorrow to bear.

Some have wept with Elizabeth and wished with all their hearts to change her state. But though we sorrow with her, we must be aware that Elizabeth received an even greater blessing than motherhood. She won, through prayer and tears, a quiet and peaceful heart when she was at last able to embrace her situation as an acceptable part of God's plan for her life.

There is probably no greater blessing in life than to be content. The apostle Paul summed it up for us in Philippians 4:11: "For I have learned, in whatsoever state I am, therewith to be content" (KJV). Elizabeth was not blessed with a child, but she found peace of heart and mind. And later God even granted her a needy child to mother and love.

Elizabeth had a husband she could respect, a sense of purpose and calling, and an active place in the church and community, so, being spiritually wise, she resolved to accept the blessings from the hand of God and to live her life fully and purposefully.

We might be tempted to envy her. She had learned the secret of happiness and contentment—a secret that seems to elude so many of us. But rather than envying her, we should resolve to find that special gift of contentment in our own heart and life.

Share with Elizabeth, through the pages of this little book, as she walked with God and learned through faith and obedience the true meaning of Christian freedom.

But godliness with contentment is great gain.
1 TIMOTHY 6:6

CONTENTS

WHEN CALLS

THE HEART

RESTLESSNESS

As I walked along on that lovely spring morning, the world appeared especially beautiful. The flower-scented air and the song of the birds made me take a rare look at my inner self.

And how are you this delightful morning? I asked myself.

Why, I am just fine, thank you, I silently answered, and then I quickly looked around for fear that someone might be able to read my thoughts. But no one shared the sidewalk with me at the moment so my self-dialogue continued.

Are you now? And what is it that makes your day so glorious—your step so feather-light?

The morning; life itself; the very fragrance of the air.

'Tis nice—but, then, you have always been a soul who took pleasure in just being alive. I do declare that you would be happy and contented anywhere on God's green earth.

No—not really. Not really.

The sudden turn of the conversation and the switch of my emotion surprised me. A strange and unfamiliar restlessness stirred deep within me. I tried to push it into a recessed corner of my being, but it elbowed its way forward.   [13–14]

A certain kind of restlessness is inevitable for believers
because we can never quite feel at home on earth.
And, like the apostle Paul, we are instructed:
both to be full and to be hungry,
both to abound and to suffer need.
PHILIPPIANS 4:12

11

CONTENTMENT

I'm not afraid of restlessness. It's just that I believe—I've been taught—that one ought to be content with what one has, especially if one has been as blessed as I. It is a shame—no, a sin—to feel discontented while enjoying all of the good things that life—and Papa—have showered upon me.

Aye, t'would be a sin to disregard one's blessings. I should never wish to do so. But perhaps, just perhaps, it would quiet my soul if I'd look fairly and squarely at what makes the empty little longing tug at me now and then.

It was a challenge; and though I still felt fearful, and perhaps not a little guilty, I knew I must take a look at this inner longing if the voice was ever to be stilled. [14]

Be content with such things as ye have:
for he hath said, I will never leave thee,
nor forsake thee.
HEBREWS 13:5

INDEPENDENCE

Our home lacked nothing. Papa provided well for us, and Mother spent hours making sure that her girls would grow into ladies. Together my parents assumed the responsibility for our spiritual nurturing and, within the proper boundaries, we were encouraged to be ourselves.

I was known as the practical one, the one who could always be counted on. It was I whom Mother called if ever there was a calamity or problem when Papa wasn't home, relying on what she referred to as my "cool head" and "quick thinking." Even at an early age I knew that she often depended on me.

I guess it was my practical side that made me prepare for independence, and with that in mind I took my training to be a teacher. I knew Mother thought that a lady, attractive and pleasant as she had raised me to be, had no need for a career; after all, a suitable marriage was available by just nodding my pretty head at some suitor. But she held her tongue and even encouraged me in my pursuit. [15–16]

Children who learn spiritual truths early
can be trusted to make wise decisions as they grow older.
Train up a child in the way he should go:
and when he is old, he will not depart from it.
PROVERBS 22:6

13

FEAR

The sweet song of a robin interrupted my morning reverie. He seemed so happy as he perched on a limb high over my head that my heart broke from its contemplation to accompany him.

By the time our song ended, I had realized that my restlessness did not come because I did not appreciate the benefits God had given me. Nor because I did not love my family. These new revelations caused some of my guilt to drain away.

But why was I feeling so restless? What was wrong with me?

Nothing is wrong, the inner me replied. *Your restlessness does not mean that you lack virtue. It is just time to move on.*

What do you think brings the robin back each spring? It is not that he no longer has his nest nor his food supply. He just knows that it is time to move on.

I had never considered moving on before. I was very much a home person. I wasn't even especially taken with the idea of marriage. And now I was to "move on." But where?

The uneasiness within me changed to a new feeling—fear. Knowing that I was not prepared to deal with these new attitudes, I pushed them from my mind. [16–17]

Fear frequently accompanies new thoughts and ideas,
but still we need to pursue them to determine whether
or not they are for our good.
*But whoso hearkeneth unto me shall dwell safely,
and shall be quiet from fear of evil.*
PROVERBS 1:33

CONFUSION

C ome and join me for tea," Mother called from the sunroom when I arrived home from school. "I got a letter from Jonathan," she announced as she handed me my cup.

Being her firstborn and only child from her first marriage, Jonathan was special to Mother. Instead of passing the letter to me as she normally did, she began to read it aloud. Jonathan's words coming from my mother's lips sent me reeling. Was he proposing that I move west to go bargainhunting for some western shopkeeper or backwoods rancher for a husband? What a cold, calculating way to look at marriage. And even if that wasn't his intent, even if he was simply looking for more teachers, why would I want to leave the perfectly good teaching position I already had? Surely Mother must see that this is totally—And then in a flash it came to me. I was to be Mother's love-offering to Jonathan. Somehow my going west to be with him would bring comfort to her heart.

I loved my mother dearly. Never would I wish to hurt her. I couldn't blurt out that the whole idea was outlandish. I needed time to think it through and to plan some way to get out of this awkward situation without hurting her. [18–22]

Teach me, O Lord, the way of thy statutes;
and I shall keep it unto the end.
Give me understanding, and I shall keep thy law;
yea, I shall observe it with my whole heart.
PSALM 119:33–34

CONFIDENCE

Later that evening Papa knocked quietly at my door. I secretly hoped he would exclaim that the whole idea was outrageous and unthinkable, but he didn't.

"Consider it? Yes, I think you should consider it," he said. "But go? Not necessarily. Only you will be able to decide that. You know that you are loved and wanted here, but should you want this new experience, we will not hold you back. We trust you to make the right decision. Whatever you decide, we want it to be what you feel you should do. Your mother, as much as she would love to see you go to Jonathan, does not want you to feel pressured to do so if it's not what you want. She asked me to tell you that, Elizabeth. She is afraid that your loyalty and desire to please her might lead you to go for her sake. That's not enough reason to make such a life-changing decision."

"Oh, Papa! Right now I'm all butterflies. I never dreamed—"

"Don't hurry, my dear. Such a decision needs much careful thinking and praying. Your mother and I will be standing behind you. Whatever you decide . . ." [22–24]

Make me to go in the path of thy commandments;
for therein do I delight.
Incline my heart unto thy testimonies,
and not to covetousness.
PSALM 119:35–36

17

DECISION-MAKING

The next few days were full of soul searching. I was so preoccupied that I sometimes wondered if I were actually teaching my students. They didn't seem to notice any difference, so I guess I was at least going through the proper motions.

I kept wavering—which was unusual for me. One moment I would think of all those that I loved—my family, my students, my church friends—and I would inwardly cry out, "I can't go, I just can't!" The next instant I would think of that part of my family in the West. Something invisible was drawing me to the older brother whom I had never really known. I also thought of all those children without a teacher, and I knew that they, too, wished to learn. I even considered the great adventure that this new opportunity held, and I would find myself reasoning, "Why not? Maybe this is the answer to the restlessness within me. Maybe I should go . . ."

Back and forth my feelings swung, like the pendulum on our grandfather clock. After considerable debate and prayer and thought, I felt directed to Joshua 1:9: "Be strong and of a good courage; be not afraid, neither be thou dismayed: for the Lord thy God is with thee whithersoever thou goest."

I repeated the passage out loud and felt my anxieties relax into peace. I would go. [25–26]

*In the multitude of my thoughts within me
thy comforts delight my soul.*
PSALM 94:19

GOOD-BYE

Another month, and the school year came to a close. I waved good-bye to the last pupil and packed up all my books and teaching aids. Blinking back tears, I said good-bye to my fellow teachers and walked away from the school without looking back.

When Papa and I took my trunks to the freight station and I presented my belongings to the man behind the counter, the realization fully hit me that I was taking a giant step into the unknown. Somewhat dazed, I watched my trunks being carted away from the checking desk. In those trunks were my books, bedding, personal effects, and almost my entire wardrobe. A large part of my life was being routinely trundled away. For a moment, fear again tightened my throat, and I had an impulse to dash out and gather those trunks back to myself and hurry back to the familiar comfort of my own home and room. Instead, I turned quickly and almost stumbled out of the building. Papa had to break into full stride to catch up to me.

As we drove home, I again thought of what a thoughtful man I had for a father. I reached over and placed my hand on his arm. I would miss him. I wiped some tears from my eyes, murmuring something about the wind in my face.   [26-28]

I will abide in thy tabernacle for ever:
I will trust in the covert of thy wings. Selah.
For thou, O God, hast heard my vows:
thou hast given me the heritage of those that fear thy name.
PSALM 61:4–5

CHANGE

I fidgeted on the worn train seat, willing my nerves to quit jumping and my heart to quit its thunderous beating.

During my four slow-moving days and nights on the Pacific Western I gradually overcame my intense homesickness. The first three days I had missed my family to such an extent that I feared I might become ill. Slowly the ache had left, leaving in its place a hollow feeling.

When the pain left me, I found some interest in the landscape. Jonathan's descriptions had not prepared me for the emptiness, the barrenness, the vastness of it all. We seemed to travel forever, seeing hardly any people.

Finally, the train blew a long, low whistle, and we traveled past some buildings. They appeared rather new and were scattered some distance apart. The streets were not cobblestoned, but dusty and busy. The train jerked to a stop with a big hiss from within its iron innards. I too sighed as I stood and gathered my things from the seat. Working my way toward the door in the slow-moving line of fellow passengers, I couldn't keep my eyes from the windows. It was all so new, so different. Was I ready to step out of the relative safety of the train and into a strange, new world? [29–32]

> *Keep sound wisdom and discretion. . .*
> *Then shalt thou walk in thy way safely,*
> *and thy foot shall not stumble.*
> PROVERBS 3:21, 23

AWE

When I stepped from the train I looked up into a pair of smiling eyes that I knew immediately belonged to Jonathan. I dropped everything and threw my arms around his neck. Jonathan's embrace made me feel at home in my new surroundings.

We loaded my belongings and started for his home. Never had I seen a town like Calgary. I wanted to stare at everything.

"Calgary is a show-off, isn't it, Elizabeth? It's almost like a fantasy, don't you think?" I could only nod my agreement, too spellbound to speak.

During the drive home Jonathan told me stories about Indians, the Mounted Police, and the settling of Calgary. Then we topped a hill. Before us was the most beautiful scene I had ever beheld. I had caught glimpses of the mountains from the train, but the panorama which lay before me now was indescribable.

"That," he said, "is why I would never leave the West."

"It's beautiful beyond description," I finally managed to say. To live in the shadow of those awe-inspiring mountains was more than I had ever dreamed. A little prayer welled up within me. Thank you, God, for the unexpected. Thank you for pushing me out of my secure nest. [32–38]

> *When I consider thy heavens, the work of thy fingers,*
> *the moon and the stars, which thou hast ordained;*
> *What is man, that thou art mindful of him?*
> *and the son of man, that thou visitest him?*
> PSALM 8:3–4

FAMILY

Mary was waiting at the door when we pulled up in front of the house. She ran to meet me and pulled me into a warm embrace almost before my feet had a chance to properly settle on the ground. I was glad for the enthusiastic welcome and immediately felt I was with family.

I studied the woman who was Jonathan's wife, my sister-in-law. A wealth of reddish-brown hair was scooped rather casually in a pinned-up style. Curly wisps of it teased about her face and neck, giving her a girlish look. Her green eyes sparked with merriment, and her full mouth produced the warmest of smiles. I smiled in return.

"Oh, Elizabeth," she exclaimed, "it is so good to meet you!"

Then she hurried me toward the house to meet the children while Jonathan busied himself in gathering up my belongings.

We passed through the main hall and out a back door to a shaded yard that seemed to be filled with shouting, wiggling small bodies. These were my nieces and nephew. At once they made a dash for me; they were not at all reserved or inhibited. It did appear that they believed the coming of an aunt was a great event.

When Mary had restored order, I was able to meet each of them—William, 8; Sarah, 6; Kathleen, 4; and baby Elizabeth— in a quieter fashion.   [39–40]

God setteth the solitary in families.
PSALM 68:6

DISCIPLINE

After a quick tour of the house, the evening meal was served, and we gathered around the table. Jonathan believed that the family should share this special time of day, and so the children joined us at the table. As I watched them clamber into chairs, I wondered just what Mother would have thought of the whole event. In our home, children, even quiet, well-mannered ones, did not join the adults at the table until they had passed their twelfth, or at the earliest, tenth birthday. I also wondered how long Kathleen would be able to sit primly like a little lady. She looked like a miniature volcano about to erupt.

Jonathan's children proved to be well-behaved in spite of their high spirits, and we adults were able to converse, uninterrupted by childish outbursts. It was obvious that they had been instructed well as to how to conduct themselves.

Maybe it is wise to start them young at the family dinner table, I decided as I watched them. [40]

Correct thy son, and he shall give thee rest;
yea, he shall give delight unto thy soul.
PROVERBS 29:17

REBUKE

I have a whole list of young men waiting to meet you," Jonathan teased. "I finally gave up trying to keep track of who was to be first. I told them—"

"I'm quite happy to meet your friends," I interrupted, "but I do want to make one thing clear. I came west to teach, not to wed. Had I been interested in matrimony, I could have stayed in the East and found an acceptable spouse."

As I continued my rather long speech, the faces of the listeners changed from unbelief, to concern, to amusement.

"I see that we shouldn't tease you so," Jonathan said. "Here we often forget the manners that our mothers tried to instill in us. We tease and jest all the time. It helps to smooth the road. Of course we have no intention of marrying you off." Then he added with sincerity, "But I could this night introduce you to a dozen good, clean, well-bred gentlemen who would make your Eastern dandies pale in comparison. But I won't do it," he hurried on, "lest my intentions be misconstrued."

I knew exactly what he was implying and realized with embarrassment that I deserved this mild rebuke for my tactlessness and bad manners. I knew I should apologize, but I couldn't get the words through my tight throat.

Jonathan chuckled, and the sound of his soft laugh eased the tension around the table.   [40–41]

Rebuke a wise man, and he will love thee.
PROVERBS 9:8

ADVICE

As I sat down in the hotel dining room I could see and feel stares following me. I smiled at my brother, pretending to be at ease so that I might feel less edgy. It worked, at least in part. Jon took over and soon I felt quite relaxed. I was becoming quite attached to my brother. No wonder Mother idolized him. I wished that she could see him here, with his lovely wife and well-behaved children, with his prestigious position in the community. She would be so proud. I also felt proud as I sat opposite him, and momentarily I was able to forget the stares.

"By the way," he said cautiously, "your clothes are lovely. Mary thinks so too. But Mary—even though she envies you, she—well—she suggested that I hint, tactfully, that you should have a few more practical things for teaching. Our classrooms are not fancy, and well—, I'm not good at hinting so . . ."

I laughed. Jon looked relieved.

"Whew," he said, "I'm glad that you took it that way. I wasn't sure whether you'd be annoyed or hurt. I'm no good at beating 'round the bush. But Mary is right; your clothing looks marvelous, but it's not too practical for our way of living."

Jon's sincerity and sweetness took all the sting out of his words. He and Mary were right; it was love that prompted them to suggest the change in wardrobe. [51–52]

Hear counsel, and receive instruction,
that thou mayest be wise in thy latter end.
PROVERBS 19:20

FRIENDS

I hurried from the store. Jon was waiting just down the street, in conversation with another man. The gentleman to whom Jon was talking was a bit taller than Jon, which made him tall indeed. A broad-brimmed hat shaded his eyes, but I could see a strong jaw and a well-shaped nose. He had a clean-cut look, though one would certainly never consider him a "parlor-gentleman." His masculine ruggedness suggested confidence and capability. He smiled good-naturedly as he spoke, and I imagined an easy friendliness and a warm sense of humor. My slight movement must have caught his eye, for his head lifted, causing Jon to look around.

"Be right with you, Beth," Jon said. The men shook hands heartily. "Greet Phillip for us," Jon said as he placed a hand on the man's shoulder. In return Jon received a friendly slap on the back; then the man turned to me. He nodded slightly, raising his hat as he did so, allowing me a full look into his deep blue eyes. I found myself wishing to see him smile, but before I could offer one to encourage him, he turned and strode away.

I could not understand the strange stirring within me. I suddenly wished that Jon had broken his rule and introduced us. Never before had I seen a man who interested me so much. I stood staring after him like a schoolgirl. [53]

Iron sharpeneth iron;
so a man sharpeneth the countenance of his friend.
PROVERBS 27:17

ANNOYANCE

Mr. Higgins showed up a bit after two o'clock. I was hoping that he was ready to get down to business, but he wanted to take me for a drive instead. I went, reluctantly. The whole thing was annoying, and I was very glad that I had a dinner engagement that evening and could insist that I be home in plenty of time to prepare for it.

I pressed him about the school where I would be teaching, but he said he was still undecided. I reminded him that I should know soon so that I could make adequate preparations. He continued to be evasive. I noted that there was only a week until classes would commence. He replied heartily that a lot could happen in a week, then exploded in uproarious laughter. I dropped the subject.

He left me at the door and remarked how quickly the afternoon had passed. He asked to see me on Friday and boldly put a hand on my arm as he shook my hand. "I do have plans for you," he said, apparently to assure me. "I do have plans for you."

The nerve of him, I thought, as I climbed the stairs to my room. Never had I met such an obnoxious man. And to think that I was in a position where he would be my employer! I did hope that our respective duties would rarely bring us into contact with one another. [54]

Wise men lay up knowledge:
but the mouth of the foolish is near destruction.
PROVERBS 10:14

REJECTION

Y ou don't need to call me Mr. Higgins, my dear Beth," he said ingratiatingly. I was shocked at his liberty in using my first name. "It's Thomas—Tom, if you like—" His eyes filled with feeling as he looked at me, "or anything else you'd care to call me."

"Mr. Higgins," I stubbornly repeated his formal name, "I'm afraid I don't understand. We came here to discuss my school—"

"Ah, my dear. I see that I haven't made myself clear. You won't need to teach. We can be married soon and I—"

"Married?" My reply sounded almost like a shriek. "Married? What are you speaking of?"

"Don't be coy, my dear. I see no need to wait. Some may think it a bit hasty, but here in the West a man is given the privilege of deciding quickly. The marriage—"

"But I came west to teach!" I took a deep breath to calm myself. "I will not forsake teaching to—to marry you!"

It was several minutes before I convinced Mr. Higgins that I was not being coy. He couldn't believe that any woman in her right mind would reject his offer—which reveals how he henceforth rated me. [58–59]

A stone is heavy, and the sand weighty;
but a fool's wrath is heavier than them both.
PROVERBS 27:3

28

REVENGE

$\mathbf{M}$r. Higgins finally spoke. "Remember, I am the school superintendent. I hire and I fire."

"Perhaps you would rather I returned to the East. I'll just tell Jonathan—"

"How absurd," he cut in. "We've plenty of schools where teachers are needed. I'm sure that I'll be able to find a spot suitable for you."

My appointment came by letter. I was given the Pine Springs school. Enclosed was a train ticket to Lacombe.

"Where is Lacombe?"

"North," Jon said from behind his paper. "Why?"

"That's where I'm to go."

"That can't be. It's more than a hundred miles from here. It's back woods, barely opened up. There must be some mistake."

It hit me then. Mr. Higgins was seeing to it that I was a long way from Calgary. His revenge? Perhaps he was even hoping that I would refuse the placement and go whimpering back East. Well, I wouldn't.

[59–60]

Avenge not yourselves, but rather give place unto wrath:
for it is written, Vengeance is mine;
I will repay, saith the Lord.
ROMANS 12:19

FINDING GOODNESS

Jon looked hurt when I told him I wanted to take the position. I hurried to explain. "I'll hate to leave you, and Mary, and the children. I've learned to love you all so. But it'll be good for me. Can't you see? I've been so sheltered. I'd like to find out if I can care for myself, if I can stand on my own."

"You're sure?" Jon looked at my carefully groomed hair, my soft hands and manicured nails, at my stylish clothes.

I understood his look. "I'm sure," I said emphatically.

"I'm still not convinced, but if you think——"

"Oh, I do. I really want to try it, Jon."

Jon's newspaper went back up to indicate that he considered the issue closed.

"Say, I just thought of something," said Jon, coming out from behind his paper again. "Pine Springs is Wynn's country."

"Who?"

"Wynn, the fellow you saw me talking to the other day when you did your shopping. Remember?"

I tried to sound nonchalant. "Oh, yes, I believe I recall the one you mean." I could feel the excitement warming my cheeks. I was glad that Jon was behind his paper again.   [60–61]

> People who try to "do us in"
> may sometimes be doing us a favor.
>> *Ye thought evil against me;*
>> *but God meant it unto good.*
>> GENESIS 50:20

ALONE

Here we are," Pearlie's father called above the roar of the motor. I must have shown my bewilderment, for he boomed at me, "The teacherage—where you'll be stayin'."

Teacherage? I gathered my thoughts and baggage together and crawled from the car. My companions did not move.

"I don't have a key!" I wailed through the window.

"A key?" He acted as if he had never heard of such an object.

"Yes, a key to let myself in the house."

"Won't need no key. Doesn't have a lock. Good-day, ma'am." He tipped his hat, pushed the shift lever into gear, and the auto clattered and chugged its way out of the yard.

I watched them go. Pearlie waved wildly, and I lifted my hand in a limp salute. I gathered my parcels and tried the door. It opened readily, and I entered my new home.

I had expected that I would be a boarder in some neighborhood home. A funny little fear rippled through me. But I told myself not to be silly, that living alone would be much more to my liking. [68–69]

Being alone does not necessarily mean being lonely.
In solitude we are more likely to hear God's sweetest songs.

And when he had sent the multitudes away,
he went up into a mountain apart to pray:
and when the evening was come,
he was there alone.
MATTHEW 14:23

31

KINDNESS

I looked around me and crossed over to some things set on the table. A note caught my eye, and I stopped to read it.

Dear Miss

Thot that you'd be tired and hungry after yer trip so have left some things. We will call on you tomorra to see what you be needing. We hope you like it here. We are plenty glad to have you come.

Martha Laverly

On the table sat containers of tea, sugar, coffee and salt, as well as cheese, fresh bread and pound cake. In the cupboard I found a collection of mismatched dishes and pots. I lifted out a brown teapot and brewed myself a cup of tea.

When my tea was ready, I sliced a piece of the fresh bread and spread on the butter, then cut myself a generous portion of cheese. Crossing to the stuffed chair, I sat down with my repast. How good the hot tea and the fresh bread tasted. I couldn't remember ever having a more enjoyable meal. [70–71]

Showing kindness to others is one of the
nicest things we can do for ourselves.
And be ye kind one to another, tenderhearted, forgiving one
another, even as God for Christ's sake hath forgiven you.
EPHESIANS 4:32

So I won't be boarding, I told myself again. *I'll be living completely on my own, in this little pioneer house.*

I returned to the lumpy chair and poured myself a fresh cup of tea. I looked around at my small, secondhand nest, feeling deep respect for the people who had worked so hard and sacrificed so much to bring me here. The sense of near-panic left me and a warm kinship with these pioneers began to seep into my mind and emotions. I felt almost happy as I thought about my still-unknown neighbors.

I will love your children, and I will teach them to the very best of my ability, I decided then and there.

I smiled to myself and sipped the hot tea. I said aloud, "Thank you, Mr. Higgins. You couldn't have given me a more pleasant situation."

[71–72]

Sometimes it is tempting to try to motivate people
through fear and intimidation, but love and kindness
are always more effective.
We love him because he first loved us.
1 JOHN 4:19

PEACE

I spent the remainder of the daylight exploring the yard around my new domain and did not return to the teacherage until the sun had retired for the night. The sunset was a splendid display. I wondered if it was showing off for my benefit or if it was often that spectacular. Rarely had I seen such a gorgeous scene; the riotous colors flamed out over the sky in shades that I had no words to describe.

Birds sang their last songs of the day before tucking in for the night, and still the darkness hung back. Now, I thought, I understand the word *twilight*. It was created for just this time— in this land.

The air began to cool, and the darkness at last started its descent. I slowly began picking my way toward my small haven, wanting to sing aloud the song that reverberated in my heart, yet holding myself in check.

This new world was so peaceful, so harmonious.   [73–74]

The peacefulness of God's creation reminds us of the spiritual peace we have when we live in obedience to Him.

Great peace have they which love thy law:
and nothing shall offend them.
PSALM 119:165

FRIGHT

As I lingered by a window of the school building, taking one last peek into the dark interior, a blood-curdling, spinechilling howl rent the stillness. It tore through my veins, leaving me terrified and shaking. The scream had hardly died away when another followed, to be joined by another.

A wolf pack! And right in my very yard! They had smelled new blood and were moving in for the kill.

I sprang forward and ran for the door of my cabin, praying that somehow God would hold them back until I was able to gain entrance. My feet tangled in the new-mown grass, and I fell to my hands and knees. With a cry, I scurried madly on. The sharp stubble of the grass and weeds bit into the palms of my hands, but I kept crawling.

Howls seemed to be all around me now. Starting as a howl, they would end in a whole chorus. I was certain they were discussing my coming end. [74]

> *Be not afraid of sudden fear. . .*
> *For the Lord shall be thy confidence,*
> *and shall keep thy foot from being taken.*
> PROVERBS 3:25–26

PREPARATION

Somehow I reached the door and scrambled inside. With trembling fingers I fastened the hook on the door and rushed into the kitchen. What would deter them? Fire. That was it. Fire would hold them back.

I rushed to the stove. It was cold and flameless. My fingers fumbled with the match as a new burst of howls split the air. The paper finally began to flame, and I thrust the kindling carelessly on top of it. I placed the lid on the stove. To my dismay there was then no evidence of fire except the small amount of warmth beginning to radiate from it. I removed the lid again and fed the flames more wood. Smoke began to fill the room. I continued to feed the fire and huddle over it, coughing and crying into the woodsmoke.

How I wish I had studied more about the habits of wilderness creatures. It had been foolish of me to venture into the wilds unprepared. I didn't even have a gun or know how to use one. [74–76]

It is wise to make provision for physical safety,
but it is even more important to make provision
for the safety of the soul.
And fear not them which kill the body,
but are not able to kill the soul:
but rather fear him which is able to destroy
both soul and body in hell.
MATTHEW 10:28

37

DEFENSELESSNESS

The minutes ticked by, and I struggled to find some way to insure my survival. *The lamp*, I thought suddenly. *It might do as a fire substitute.*

I fumbled in the darkened room until I found the lamp and the matches. When the small flame flickered, I beheld a room blue with smoke. No wonder I was having trouble breathing.

I looked around the room. There was nothing available for my defense, and it was very late. No one would be going by on the road at this hour. I ached with tiredness and fear, and my hands and knees stung from their scratches and bruises. Suddenly it dawned on me that there was nothing I could do to defend myself, and that I was foolish to pretend that I could.

I placed more wood in the stove, set my lighted lamp on the table by the window, and went to my bedroom. I closed the curtain and slipped my soiled dress and one of my petticoats over my head. Without bothering to find my nightgown, I lay down on the sheetless bed and pulled the quilt over my head.

"Lord," I prayed, "I've done all that I know to do. You'll have to take over now." [77–78]

> Houses, weapons, and our own wits give us
> an illusion of safety and help us feel secure,
> but in the end, our only security is God.
> *Because of his strength will I wait upon thee:*
> *for God is my defence.*
> PSALM 59:9

PRAISE

When I awoke the next morning, my fear was gone, but pain and stiffness reminded me of my terrifying evening. I cleaned myself as well as I could and opened the windows to clear the air. I had barely put things in order when a young boy with a shy grin came to my door.

"Hello," he said, "Ma sent me over to help ya."

I shared my breakfast with him while we got acquainted.

"What do people around here do about the wolves, Lars?" I eventually asked, trying to hide my concern.

"Volves?" He looked surprised. "Ve don't got no volves."

"But last night I heard them."

"Oh, dem's coyotes. Silly ole coyotes. Pa says coyotes are yella-livered. Scared of der own shadows."

"They never attack people?"

"Not coyotes. Dey're scared silly of everyt'ing—especially people. As soon as you git a little close, dey run vid der tails 'tveen der legs as fast as dey can go."

Humiliation flushed my cheeks. Coyotes—harmless, noisy coyotes.   [79–83]

Sometimes our worst fears are based on
misunderstanding or misinformation.
But I will sing of thy power; yea, I will sing aloud
of thy mercy in the morning: for thou hast been
my defence and refuge in the day of my trouble.
PSALM 59:16

LONELINESS

When Mr. Laverly learned that I did not have my trunks, he kindly offered to take me to town. I accepted, grateful for the opportunity to retrieve my belongings and to purchase some of the items my new home was lacking.

When we returned to the teacherage, Mr. Laverly unloaded all my belongings, and I spent the rest of the day getting settled. As dusk approached, I gazed around me with pleasure. It looked and felt much more like home now.

While my bath water heated, I fixed a simple meal and then drank a cup of tea from my new teacup. Staring at the matching cup, I wondered if there would ever be a second person in my little teacherage to share my teatime. Suddenly a wave of loneliness overtook me. I was happy here, but I was alone. I longed for my sister, Julie, and then realized that even she would not fill the void. I needed someone with serenity, strength, and purposefulness to share my thoughts and my days. My mind involuntarily began to rehearse the men I had known. I readily dismissed each face that appeared. Then suddenly, without warning, I saw again the face of Jon's friend. His intense eyes, slight smile, and evident strength of character attracted me and yet made me stir uneasily. I quickly changed my thoughts to less foolish things and set about preparing my bath.   [91–93]

For he satisfieth the longing soul,
and filleth the hungry soul with goodness.
PSALM 107:9

JOY

When I awoke the next morning, I felt stiff all over. I was tempted to stay under the covers, but my body would not allow me the privilege. I thought of the small structure marked "Girls" way across the clearing and wondered if my legs would be able to walk the distance. I did wish they had thought to build it nearer the teacherage.

I dressed clumsily and started walking slowly. The sun was up and shining down on a picture-pretty world. By the time I had traveled across to the building and back, some of the kinks were loosening. I decided I would be able to face the day after all.

While I waited for the water to heat for my morning coffee, I took my Bible and turned to the passage in Nehemiah where I had been reading. Though Nehemiah was leading a whole nation and rebuilding a city, I found some exciting parallels between his story and my new life way out here in the Canadian frontier. The day suddenly seemed to hold great promise. Before I finished my prayer the kettle was singing merrily. [94]

It is of the Lord's mercies that we are not consumed,
because his compassions fail not.
They are new every morning: great is thy faithfulness.
LAMENTATIONS 3:22–23

GRATITUDE

I spent the morning carrying books and classroom aids to the little schoolhouse, then made a quick lunch and spent the afternoon organizing things. I even wrote a few simple adding exercises on the blackboard. I hung the alphabet and number charts, put up some study pictures and maps, and the room began to come alive.

Around five o'clock, while I was still lingering in the classroom choosing Psalms to read for the opening on Monday morning, I heard the jingle of a harness. It was Mr. Johnson delivering the tables and benches. He had a grown son with him who took one look at me and went red to the very roots of his hair. I pretended not to notice, to save him further embarrassment, and showed them where to place the furniture. Mr. Johnson gazed around the classroom. Tears began to gather in his eyes and trickle down his creased cheeks.

"Da Lord be praised!" he exclaimed. "It really be so. Ve do haf school. Yah?"

His deep feelings touched me. [94–95]

> *I will praise thee, O Lord, with my whole heart;*
> *I will shew forth all thy marvellous works.*
> *I will be glad and rejoice in thee:*
> *I will sing praise to thy name,*
> *O thou most High.*
> PSALM 9:1–2

RULES

$\mathbf{A}$fter writing "My name is Miss Thatcher" in block letters on the blackboard, I reluctantly turned to go home.

As I walked toward the door, I noticed a printed list posted beside it. I had not spotted it before. It was captioned "Rules for the Teacher." My eyes ran quickly down the page.

1. A teacher may not marry during the school year.
2. Lady teachers are not to keep company with men.
3. Lady teachers must be home between the hours of 8:00 p.m. and 6:00 a.m.
4. Man teachers must not chew tobacco.
5. There must be no loitering, by male or female, in downtown stores or ice-cream parlors.
6. A teacher may not travel outside the district limits without permission from the school-board chairman.
7. Neither male nor female may smoke.
8. Bright colors are not to be worn.

There were fourteen in all. I didn't expect to have any trouble obeying the lengthy list, but it bothered me to be dictated to in such a fashion.

[95–96]

Rules and laws are not always the best way
to encourage good behavior.
Ye have been called unto liberty; only use not liberty
for an occasion to the flesh, but by love serve one another.
GALATIANS 5:13

FELLOWSHIP

There wasn't any reason for my early rising on Sunday except perhaps habit. After I had carefully dressed and groomed my hair, I fussed about my small kitchen, fixing myself a special breakfast, as had been our tradition at home on Sunday mornings.

After I had cleared away the mess I had managed to make, I went outside for a walk. The sunshine felt good on my shoulders and back. I wanted to lie down in the grass and let the warm rays do for me what my inadequate tub had been unable to do.

The morning hours seemed to lag. Eventually I returned to the house, hoping that my clock would tell me it was time to prepare my noon meal. I was still plenty early, but I started the preparations anyway.

In the afternoon I read more about Nehemiah and spent time in prayer. I missed, more than I had ever thought possible, our church back home. I should have thought to ask the Petersons if there was a church nearby where I might meet on Sundays with other believers. I couldn't imagine living without an opportunity for worship and fellowship. How dry the endless days would become with no Sunday service to revive and refresh one's spirit. [97-98]

We took sweet counsel together,
and walked unto the house of God in company.
PSALM 55:14

LEARNING

Is dat all da books?" Else pointed at my Bible and the book of poetry with which I had attempted to fill my day.

"Oh, no. I have no bookshelves, so I had to leave my books in the trunk." I raised the lid to show her the volumes that had become my good friends over the years. Her eyes caressed them.

"Maybe you'd like to see the school. I took the books for classroom use over there." Else and Lars flashed excited glances at each other, so together we walked to the school.

First they stopped and stared, their eyes traveling over everything. Lars began to softly name the letters on the alphabet chart, while Else migrated toward the meager stacks of primers and books at the front of the room. I went with her and lifted a book from the others. "Here, try this one," I encouraged her.

She took the book and gently turned each page, missing nothing as her eyes eagerly drank in the pictures and her mind sought for the words on the printed pages.

If I had been in doubt about teaching in a one-room classroom with students who had never had any formal learning, I would have lost all such doubts after seeing their response to the school. I knew that Monday held great promise.   [100–101]

Yea, if thou criest after knowledge, and liftest up thy voice for understanding. . .; Then shalt thou understand the fear of the Lord, and find the knowledge of God. For the Lord giveth wisdom: out of his mouth cometh knowledge and understanding.
PROVERBS 2:3, 5–6

BUSYNESS

The week was a busy one. I arose early each morning to write assignments on the blackboard and to add last-minute ideas to the lessons that I had prepared. The day was given entirely to the students. Daily I felt frustrated by my lack of materials for teaching. *If only I had. . .*, I often started thinking. But I didn't have, so I tried to make up for the lack with creativity.

At the end of the classroom time, I lingered for a few moments to correct work and plan the next day, then rushed home, made my cup of tea, and rested for a few moments in my overstuffed chair. All the time I sipped, my mind refused to relax. It leaped from one idea to another, from plan to plan. As soon as my cup was empty I returned to work in the classroom, trying to put my ideas to work.

By the end of the week I was physically weary, but I was perhaps the happiest I had ever been in my life. [105]

The hand of the diligent shall bear rule:
but the slothful shall be under tribute.
PROVERBS 12:24

Seest thou a man diligent in his business?
he shall stand before kings.
PROVERBS 22:29

ACCEPTANCE

Mr. Dickerson was in charge of the Sunday afternoon service at the school. We sang several songs and read scripture. Mrs. Thebeau gave a Bible lesson for the children, then Mr. Dickerson gave some thoughts on a passage of scripture. It was *not* a sermon, he clarified, because he was *not* a preacher. He voiced some worthwhile insights, and I appreciated his direct approach. I even found myself thinking that it was a shame he was *not* a preacher.

As we stood around visiting after the short service, other teams began pulling into the schoolyard. I glanced about me. To my surprise there was activity going on all around me. Seeing my puzzled look, Anna Peterson crossed over to me.

"Da folks wanta meet da new teacher. Dis be gud vay, yah?"

I was astounded. But as the afternoon went on I agreed with Anna. Yes, this was a good way. They all welcomed me heartily. I liked my new neighbors. In comparison to my upbringing, they lacked refinement and polish; but they were open and friendly, and I respected their spirit of venture and their sense of humor. They were hearty people, these pioneers. They knew how to laugh and, obviously, they knew how to work.   [113–114]

God's boundless creativity resulted in endless diversity. Therefore, those who are different are not necessarily wrong.

If ye have respect of persons, ye commit sin.
JAMES 2:9

DISAPPOINTMENT

I was tidying up the room when I heard a rap on the door. Wynn Delaney walked in. As usual, his presence unnerved me.

"Am I interrupting?" he asked.

"Not at all. I was just leaving. Please come in."

Mr. Delaney's relaxed attitude put me more at ease, and I began to enjoy his company.

"Tell me, Miss Thatcher, how did Phillip respond to having to stay late to finish his work? Did it upset him?"

"Not at all," I said, becoming defensive.

He smiled—slowly and deliberately. Though pleasant, his smile told me that he had just proved a point. He didn't say anything; he just waited for me to understand.

"You mean. . .?" I began slowly.

"Exactly. He likes nothing better than the extra attention."

"I see," I said. "So, what do you suggest?"

"Well, his mother and I—"

His mother and I. The words hit me like a pail of cold water. I felt the air leaving my lungs and the blood draining from my head. So Wynn Delaney was Phillip's father. What a fool I'd been to assume he was unmarried. I struggled to regain my composure.   [124–126]

Without counsel purposes are disappointed:
but in the multitude of counsellors they are established.
PROVERBS 15:22

GROWING UP

Sally Clark found a warm place in my heart. She was rather pathetic, this girl-turning-woman. She wanted so much to enter the adult world, yet she clung to her childish world as well.

I noticed, as the days went by, her awkward attempts to copy me. I took it as a compliment, and I often wished I could take her home with me, put her in one of my pretty dresses, arrange her hair, and then let her see the attractive girl in the mirror.

She was a pretty girl, and I often thought that someday we might waken and find this shy little butterfly free of her cocoon. I realized that I would be unwise to try and rush nature's own slow, yet certain, process. To show Sally my wardrobe and tempt her with pretty things would only make her worn and simple clothing look all the more drab. So, rather, I made simple suggestions and encouraged her when I could: "Blue is one of your best colors"; "That type of collar suits you well"; "Your hair looks very pretty that way—you have such pretty hair."

I tried to build up each one of my pupils with sincere praise, but with Sally my smiles and words had extra meaning. She flushed slightly when I did this, but I knew that my approval was important to her. [128]

Therefore encourage one another and build each other up.
1 THESSALONIANS 5:11 NIV

DOING GOOD

Then there was Andy. He wanted to learn, but he couldn't remember much. He had been kicked by a horse when he was three years old. The side of his head bore a vicious scar. I longed to find some way to protect him from the cruel, angry world. Even to look at him made my heart ache. At times I saw him reach up and grasp his head with both hands as though he were in pain, a look of confusion and misery filling his eyes.

One morning Andy's sister, Teresa, arrived without him. "Mamma think he need rest," she explained, and I nodded my head in sympathetic agreement.

All the students missed Andy. Even though he could not fully participate, he vigorously cheered those who could. His eyes would shine whenever anyone read or recited well, and occasionally he spontaneously clapped his hands in jolly appreciation. I never reproached him for his exuberance, and the students watched Andy as they recited, hoping to win his favor. On the playground he watched the games with intent, and shouted and jumped wildly for any accomplishment. Andy did not pick favorites. He cheered everyone with the same enthusiasm. His clapping hands and fervent exclamation of "You did good! You did good!" were two things every student worked for. [128–129]

Those who suffer the most,
often know the most about God's goodness.
Be not overcome of evil, but overcome evil with good.
ROMANS 12:21

DETERMINATION

Considering the fact that my students had never had any formal education prior to this year; considering the fact that I had very few educational aids to use on their behalf; considering the fact that I had all of them under one roof and on all grade levels; considering the fact that they came from various ethnic backgrounds, and some of them did not even speak English well; considering the fact that I was young with only two previous years of teaching experience, I was pleased with nearly everyone's progress.

Over the weeks I was invited to several neighborhood homes for Sunday dinner or a weekday supper. Some of the homes I visited were even more simply furnished than my little teacherage. A few were surprisingly comfortable and charmingly decorated and arranged. But wherever I went, the people were anxious to share with me the best they could offer. I loved them for it.

It was difficult for me to accept their hospitality when I was not in a position to return it. They seemed to sense how I felt and were quick to assure me that this was their small way of saying thanks to me for coming to teach their children. It made me more determined than ever to do the best that I could.

[130–131]

And let us consider one another to provoke
unto love and to good works.
HEBREWS 10:24

SMALL THINGS

When I reached into my drawer I sensed that something was wrong—seriously wrong. Then I realized what had happened. The mice had been at my handkerchiefs. With a cry I pulled them out and stared at them. Pretty lace and embroidery had been reduced to chewed fragments. My favorite had suffered the worst. Tears gathered in my eyes and rolled down my cheeks. This time the mice had gone too far. Tonight I would tell Mr. Laverly that I could not live in the teacherage until these despicable rodents were eliminated.

Mr. Laverly listened patiently to my problem but I gathered that he didn't feel that a few mice were anything to get so worked up about. He offered to get me some traps. I explained that I had tried not only traps but a cat as well and that neither had worked. Finally he promised to get rid of the destructive creatures for me. We agreed that I would stay with the Petersons for a week while he and his sons dealt with the mice.

"You'd better enjoy yourselves tonight," I warned the varmints when I returned home. "It might be your last chance."

From the evidence I found the next morning, it appeared they had.   [141–147]

Sometimes the smallest "varmints,"
the ones that remain unseen, do the most damage.
Who can understand his errors?
Cleanse me from secret faults.
PSALM 19:12

CONCERN

My students' concern for Andy led them to action. With help from their parents we planned a box social to raise money to send Andy to the doctor in Calgary. Our total earnings, including donations from neighbors, came to $195.64. A cheer went up when I announced the sum.

"We all love Andy," I continued, "and I would like to ask Mr. Dickerson to lead us in prayer on Andy's behalf."

A silence fell over the room. Eyes filled with tears, heads bowed, and calloused hands reached up to sweep hats aside. Mr. Dickerson's simple and sincere prayer was followed by whispered "Amens."

Andy's family was the last to leave. Mr. Pastachuck shook my hand firmly. His wife could only smile through tears, unable to speak. But Andy looked at me with shining eyes, as though to herald a personal triumph on my behalf. "It was fun," he exclaimed. "You did good, Teacher, real good!"

I reached down and pulled him close, holding him for a long time. Then, without another word, he brushed the tears from my cheek.

[158]

*Inasmuch as ye have done it unto one of the least of these
my brethren, ye have done it unto me.*
MATTHEW 25:40

DEATH

The students and I wrote notes to Andy telling him that we prayed for him daily in our opening prayers, that we missed him, and that we would be glad when he was well enough to be back with us.

But Andy did not return. He died during surgery. On Wednesday afternoon we all gathered at the schoolhouse for his short funeral service. It was a short distance to the cemetery so we walked to it. The little procession with its small pine casket at the head stirred up little pillowy swirls of dust. The day was bright, the autumn sun glistening in a tranquil sky. A few clouds skittered across the blueness. The leaves still clinging to the trees were in full dress, but many others lay scattered on the ground, rustling at each stirring of the breeze.

"Andy would have liked this day," Else whispered, looking up at its brightness. I knew that she was right. I could imagine the gentle little boy with his shining eyes cheering this day on.

"You did good," he would exclaim to the beautiful morning. "You did good." [159–160]

Yea, though I walk through the valley of the shadow of death,
I will fear no evil: for thou art with me;
thy rod and thy staff they comfort me.
PSALM 23:4

I cried then, the great sobs shaking my whole body. I remembered the last time that I had wept and how the little boy in my embrace had reached up awkwardly, yet tenderly, to brush away my tears. "You did good, Teacher," he had whispered. And now that small boy had passed beyond—so young to journey on alone.

But then I remembered that he hadn't traveled alone—not one step of the way—for as soon as the loving hands had released him here, another Hand had reached out to gently take him. I tried to visualize him entering that new Land, the excitement and eagerness shining forth on his face, the cheers rising from the shrill little voice. There would be no pain twisting his face now, no need to hold his head and rock back and forth. Joy and happiness would surround him.

I could almost hear his words as he looked at the glories of heaven and gave the Father his jubilant ovation—"You did good, God. You did real good!" [160]

> *In my Father's house are many mansions. . . .*
> *I go to prepare a place for you.*
> *And if I go and prepare a place for you,*
> *I will come again, and receive you unto myself;*
> *that where I am, there ye may be also.*
> JOHN 14:2–3

TRUTH

We closed school for the rest of the week following Andy's funeral, so I went to visit Jon and his family. Kathleen was excited because her beloved Dee was coming for dinner.

Kathleen's "one and only" turned out to be Wynn Delaney. "I'm gonna marry you when I grow up," Kathleen said, pointing a finger at his broad chest. "Right?"

"I don't suppose so." He spoke very carefully. "People can be very special to one another—and not marry. For instance, you love your daddy very much, but you don't need to marry him to share that love, do you?"

Kathleen shook her head slowly, her initial disappointment dissipating a bit.

"Well, that's like us. We are very special to one another, but we don't need to be married to stay special."

Dee had been quite convincing. Kathleen bounced down from the lounge, her troubled eyes shining again.

"You could have humored her a bit," scolded Nanna, Kathleen's grandmother. "She's only a child. She would discover the truth as she grew older."

Mr. Delaney became serious. "If anyone deserves the truth, a child does. They can accept even hurtful things, if they are dealt with honestly, in love." [165–166]

Speaking the truth in love,
we will in all things grow up into him.
EPHESIANS 4:15 NIV

MISUNDERSTANDING

His words hung about my head, making me angry. How could he say such things when he himself was living a horrible lie. I excused myself from the room and headed for my bedroom. I feared that I was going to be sick.

Mary found me a few minutes later.

"Dee was worried about you, Beth. Is something wrong?"

"Mary, didn't you tell me that Wynn Delaney is unmarried?"

"Yes."

"Well, maybe the reason he hasn't taken a Calgary wife is that he already has one."

"Wynn?" Mary queried. "That's impossible. We've known Wynn—"

"Well, apparently you don't know him very well. He has a wife and son. I've met them. His son, Phillip, is my student."

"Elizabeth, Phillip is Lydia and Phillip's child. Wynn is the senior Phillip's brother. The reason Wynn is in Calgary so often is that Phillip is in the hospital, and that's why Wynn is staying with Lydia and Phillip."

My knees felt weak. I groped behind me for the bed and sat down. I thought of the many times I had been rude—inexcusably so—to Wynn. How could I ever make things right? Now I *knew* I was going to be sick.   [166-168]

He that is slow to wrath is of great understanding:
but he that is hasty of spirit exalteth folly.
PROVERBS 14:29

APOLOGY

I owe you an explanation," I began in a quavering voice when Wynn and I were alone. "You see, I thought you were Phillip's father. And Lydia's husband."

His jaw dropped. "But how?" He shook his head in disbelief. "Where did you ever get such an idea?"

He was questioning, not accusing, but I was on the defensive. Surely it wasn't all my stupidity. Tears stung my eyes.

"I got the idea," I said, with emphasis, "because *you* were living in the same house as Lydia, *you* came to school about Phillip's homework, *you* spoke of 'his mother and I,' and *you* shared the same last name."

"I see. So that's why you wouldn't eat your box lunch with me," he chuckled. "It's really rather funny. I spend ten dollars and sixty-five cents so I can sit with the pretty schoolteacher and instead I eat alone because she thinks——"

"You spent how much?" I interrupted. The other boxes were going for one or two——"

"I know," he smiled. "But it was a good buy. Besides, it *was* a good cause, so I don't begrudge the money."

Having nothing more to offer than my insufficient apology, I excused myself. I needed to contemplate the meaning of this unexpected revelation. [171–174]

Confess your faults to one another,
and pray one for another.
JAMES 5:16

PRIORITIES

So, what do you think of our Dee—now that you've allowed him his rightful single status?" Mary asked the next day.

"He's very nice." My words sounded silly, but I couldn't think of anything more appropriate to say.

"He's more than nice. He's very special. I had even dared to hope—" Then, changing her mind in mid-sentence, she said, "Just wish he weren't so stubborn. He's got this crazy notion that marriage and his work do not go together. He's determined that he will *never* ask a woman to share his life with him. He says that the order of his life must be God, work, wife, and he won't ask a woman to take the lesser position."

"My, my," I said, trying to sound casual and even a bit sarcastic, "he must be a *very* special man."

"He doesn't think *he's* special. He just thinks his job with the Royal Canadian Mounted Police is. He's totally dedicated to it. It takes him into some primitive settings, and he says he won't ask a woman to share that."

"But if a woman really loved a man surely she wouldn't mind. Doesn't he know there is such a thing as love?"

"Little Beth," Mary said, her eyes twinkling, "maybe you'll have to show him." [175–176]

Love suffereth long, and is kind; love envieth not;
love vaunteth not itself, is not puffed up,
doth not behave itself unseemly, seeketh not her own.
1 CORINTHIANS 13:4–5

BELONGING

On Monday morning I wanted to spend time in the local library to search out some information I needed in my teaching. I asked Jon if he would drive me downtown well before train time. He delivered me to the station where we purchased my ticket and left my suitcase with the clerk. I bid Jon good-bye, trying hard to explain just how much the weekend had meant to me. I felt ready to return to my classroom.

I walked the short distance to the library and began to browse through the titles. It was a small library so I did not bother asking for help but went looking on my own. My eyes caught a rather unusual title, *The Origin and Meaning of Names.* I pulled it from the shelf and flipped through the pages. I found "Elizabeth." It was Hebrew, the book said, and meant "consecrated to God." The meaning pleased me. It was nice to belong to Him. [177]

Ye have received the Spirit of adoption,
whereby we cry, Abba, Father.
The Spirit itself beareth witness with our spirit,
that we are the children of God:
And if children, then heirs;
heirs of God, and joint-heirs with Christ.
ROMANS 8:15–17

CHRISTMAS

When I returned to Calgary, it was Christmastime. We spent the first few days of my visit shopping, baking, decorating, and preparing for Christmas. On Christmas Eve we attended a special service that brought to mind the wonder of the first Christmas. God had sent His most precious gift, His Son Jesus, into the world to be born of a woman so that someday, as a sacrifice, He could provide salvation for the whole human race.

The familiar Christmas carols had never meant so much to me. As I sang the words, I pictured the young Mary, her hour having come, with no one to care for her—no warm bed, no private room, no skilled midwife—only straw, a stable, and an anxious husband nearby. She herself cared for the newborn Son of God, the baby Jesus.

I thought of my Lord, the Maker of Heaven and Earth, now reduced to a helpless child, not even able to express His needs and wants, far less demand the honor due Him; and I thought of the Father who must have watched anxiously from His throne as the new Babe made His appearance in the world that He had fashioned. God himself lay snuggled against the breast of a young peasant girl in a dimly lit stable in Bethlehem. How God must have loved mankind to allow Him to come. [188–190]

For God so loved the world, that he gave
his only begotten Son, that whosoever believeth in him
should not perish, but have everlasting life.
JOHN 3:16

DECEIT

On Christmas day the children begged to try their new sleds. Wynn and I accompanied Jon and the children to the hill. After a few breathless rides and long return climbs, I rested against a tree and enjoyed the sparkling freshness of the winter air.

"Jon said I should take you to the top of the ridge and show you the mountains," Wynn announced.

"Oh," I cried, "can you see them from here?"

The loose snow made climbing difficult, but the view was worth every step. Stretched out before us, the snow-capped peaks of the magnificent Rockies glistened in the winter sun.

"I wish I could take you there someday, Elizabeth, but—"

Reluctantly I started down the slope. My thoughts were on Wynn's unfinished sentence, not on where I was placing my feet. Suddenly my ankle twisted beneath me. My injury was not serious, but I allowed Wynn to examine it when he insisted.

"Nothing broken," he assured me as he swept me into his arms, "but I'd better carry you to avoid aggravating it." When he set me down, I had to look to see which boot had the untied laces to remember which foot I had injured.

For the rest of the evening I feigned a limp. When bedtime came I was relieved to take my perfectly fine ankle, and my guilty conscience, to the privacy of my own room.   [196–200]

Bread of deceit is sweet to a man;
but afterwards his mouth shall be filled with gravel.
PROVERBS 20:17

The next morning I brushed aside the inquiries about my ankle and assured everyone that it was fine. Nevertheless, to appease Mary, who insisted that I stay off my feet, I retreated to Jon's library where I buried myself in a good book.

About noon Jon entered with William in tow. Jon sat down and pulled William to him. "Now, Son, do you realize that what you've done is wrong?"

"Yes."

"Do you realize that what you've done is *sin?*"

"It's not *that* wrong."

"Oh, yes, it is. God has said, 'Thou shalt not,' but you did. Now doesn't that make it sin?"

"Well, it wasn't a very *big* sin," William argued.

"There are no 'big' or 'little' sins, Son. Sin is sin. I know you didn't mean to hurt God, so I want you to tell Him that you are sorry, and that with His help you will not do it again. After that, we will go and have a talk with Stacy."

"I'll talk to God, Pa, but can't *you* talk to Stacy?"

"No, Son. Part of being forgiven is making things right."

I never did discover what William's wrong was. It did not seem important—for pricking at my own conscience was my own dishonesty of the day before. [201–203]

> *If we confess our sins, he is faithful and just to forgive us*
> *our sins, and to cleanse us from all unrighteousness.*
> 1 JOHN 1:9

RESTORATION

Williiam appeared at the table for lunch with all traces of tears gone. In fact, he looked happier than usual, and when Stacy served the dessert I noticed that William received a larger-than-usual serving. William noticed it, and he gave Stacy a grin. She winked—ever so quickly and slyly. Repentance, confession, and restitution. William knew all about the benefits, while I still sat miserable and squirming in my chair.

After lunch I went to my room. I was like William. I didn't mind telling my wrongdoing to God, but to speak to Wynn? The very thought made my cheeks burn. Yet, plead as I would for God's forgiveness, I had no peace of heart. Confession—confession—kept ringing in my mind. Finally I threw myself upon my bed in desperation.

"Please, God, I know it was sin, but don't make me talk to Wynn. What will he think of me?"

"Do you care what God thinks of you?"

"Of course, but . . ."

I wept, I pleaded, I argued, but at length I gave in.

Peace came, but my dread of the encounter with Wynn did not go away. [203–204]

> If we say that we have fellowship with him,
> and walk in darkness, we lie, and do not the truth:
> But if we walk in the light, as he is in the light,
> we have fellowship one with another.
> 1 JOHN 1:6–7

CONFESSION

I did not need to be in misery for long. Wynn dropped by that evening to check on me. I swallowed hard and stood up. I wanted to run away, to hide my face—anything but face Wynn with the truth. Before I could do any such thing, I plunged in.

"I have a confession—about my ankle. I didn't injure it. I just pretended. It's fine." I dropped my gaze, unable to look into his honest, blue eyes. "I didn't think you would carry me. I guess I wanted your attention—and I didn't know how else to get it. I know it was foolish, and I'm sorry."

Wynn looked directly at me. His eyes did not scorn or mock me, nor did he look shocked or disgusted. There was an understanding and a softness that I had not expected.

"I have confessed my dishonesty to God and received His forgiveness. Now I would like to ask *your* forgiveness also."

"Elizabeth, I can't tell you how much I respect you for what you have just done. I give you my forgiveness, and now I must ask yours. I examined your ankle and it was my choice to carry you, right? Elizabeth, I am trained in first aid—to recognize breaks, injuries, and sprains—"

"Then—you knew?"

The twinkle of humor returned to his eyes. With a slight nod he departed, closing the door softly behind him.   [204–205]

He that covereth his sins shall not prosper:
but whoso confesseth and forsaketh them shall have mercy.
PROVERBS 28:13

LOVE

I learned much about Wynn that week: that he loved people; that he was respected—by White and Indian; that he read widely and was able to converse about science as easily as he could recite poetry; that he had a deep and solid faith in God; and that he sensed a mission to help those whom many believed to be second-rate citizens. The more I knew of him the more I admired him, and what had previously been an infatuation was daily turning into a feeling much more deep and permanent.

He was kind to me, even solicitous. He even seemed to enjoy my company, but never once did he give me reason to believe that he had changed his mind about marriage.

I couldn't understand how a man could be so stubborn, but because he was, I knew that I must try to dismiss him from my thoughts. If I hadn't already learned to love him so much, I would angrily, though painfully, have done so.   [206]

Despite our stubbornness,
God does not dismiss us from His thoughts.
Thou knowest my downsitting and mine uprising, thou
understandest my thought afar off. Thou compassest my path
and my lying down, and art acquainted with all my ways.
For there is not a word in my tongue, but lo, O Lord,
thou knowest it altogether. Thou hast beset me behind
and before, and laid thine hand upon me.
Such knowledge is too wonderful for me.
PSALM 139:2–6

HAPPINESS

The rest of the school year passed quickly, and I was forced to make a decision about the future. My determination to put Wynn from my mind had not helped me accomplish it. I thought of him constantly. I finally made up my mind to return to Toronto. Maybe there my broken heart would mend. But pulling myself away from the people who had given so much of themselves to me tore out another piece of my already wounded heart. After many days of tear-drenched good-byes it was time to make my way to the boarding platform.

"Elizabeth."

I turned and saw Wynn's troubled eyes.

"Elizabeth, I've been miserable. I've come to ask you not to go. I know it's selfish, but I must tell you—before you decide— that I love you and that I want you to be my wife."

I threw myself into his arms, tears spilling down his red tunic. My train whistled in the distance, but I didn't mind that all my belongings were on their way to Toronto. Everything I would ever need was with me this moment in Calgary.　　　　[216–221]

Though only God's love can fulfill our deepest needs,
the love between a man and woman can be an important part
of God's plan for our lives.

And the Lord God said, It is not good that the man
should be alone. . . . Therefore shall a man . . . cleave unto
his wife: and they shall be one flesh.
GENESIS 2:18, 24

WHEN COMES

THE SPRING

PERFECTION

How come it takes so many times to make a wedding dress?" Kathleen asked again.

"Because a wedding dress must be perfect," I answered.

"Per-fect?" queried Kathleen.

"Um-hum. That means 'just right'—for the man I'm going to marry."

I thought of poor Mary and of all the work that my September wedding—only eight weeks away—was causing her. How I loved her! It wasn't one bit necessary for her to fuss so, but she insisted. After all, it would be the first time her in-laws would be in her home and she, too, wanted everything to be perfect.

"Is Grandma fuzzy?" asked Kathleen seriously.

"Fussy?" I smiled but did not let Kathleen know her word had come out wrong. "Well, yes and no. Grandma likes nice things, and when she is in charge she tries very hard to see that everything is just right. But she does not judge other people by the same rules she uses on herself."

"What's that mean?"

"It means that Grandma loves people as they are. She doesn't ask for everyone to be perfect."   [11–14]

> *But let patience have her perfect work,*
> *that ye may be perfect and entire, wanting nothing.*
> JAMES 1:4

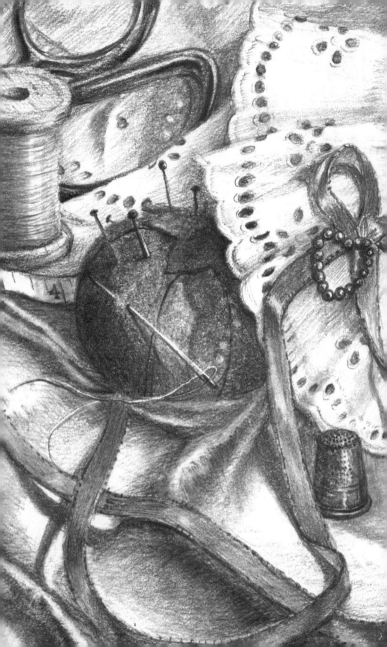

VALUES

Poor Kathleen. No wonder she's feeling left out. Everyone has something to do but her. Sarah is at Molly's house making a dress for her doll; William is working with his father at the store; Baby Elizabeth is sleeping; and Mary is sewing wedding dresses as frantically as I am.

"How would you like to take the streetcar uptown and stop at the ice cream parlor?"

Kathleen's shine was back. "Could we?" she cried.

"A little break would do me good," Mary said when I asked her about going.

I went back to my own room to change my dress. My eyes wandered to the pile of lustrous satin. I was so anxious to see the final product of all my labors. But I pushed the dress from my mind. Kathleen was more important.

I had been so busy with details of the wedding that I had not even been able to enjoy Wynn's company, I realized, looking back over some of our last evenings together. I resolved to change all that. People are more important than preparations. And a marriage is far more important than a wedding. [14–16]

Lay not up for yourselves treasures upon earth . . .
but lay up for yourselves treasures in heaven . . .
For where your treasure is, there will your heart be also.
MATTHEW 6:19–21

MEETING NEEDS

Wynn arrived a little earlier than I had expected, so Sarah let him in and Kathleen entertained him until I was ready. When I walked into the parlor Wynn was listening attentively to the chattering Kathleen, and I couldn't help but smile at the homey picture they made.

"An' after that, we went an' looked in the store windows—just for fun," explained Kathleen. "An' then we took a ride on the streetcar just as far as it would go—just to see where it went—an' then we took it back all the way home again!" Kathleen waved her small hand to show Wynn just how far all the way home really was.

Wynn smiled at the little girl. Clearly he was enjoying their conversation.

"Was it fun?" he asked. Wynn didn't need the answer, of course, but he asked because he sensed that Kathleen needed to be able to express it. [17–18]

We then that are strong
ought to bear the infirmities of the weak,
and not to please ourselves.
ROMANS 15:1

AFFECTION

The sound of the front door told us that Jonathan had arrived home. He entered the house to encounter his two young daughters talking excitedly. Jonathan tried to listen to them both, attempting to share in the excitement and the enthusiasm they felt. And William had tales of his own he was bursting to tell. He had worked just like a man at his father's business and was making great plans for all the money he was sure to make over the summer.

Mary joined the happy commotion in the hall and was greeted by her husband with a warm hug and a kiss. Jonathan did not agree with the tradition of parents hiding their affection from their children's seeing eyes.

"Who needs to know more than they that I love you?" he often said to Mary; and so the children grew up in a household where loving was an accepted and expected part of life. [19–20]

Be kindly affectioned one to another
with brotherly love;
in honour preferring one another.
ROMANS 12:10

THE IMPOSSIBLE

When Wynn and I were alone I told him of my new resolve. "We can do things much more simply. There is no need to wear ourselves out. If I put half as much effort into making a marriage work as I have put into preparing for a wedding—"

Wynn's arm tightened around me and he took a deep breath. "My posting came today. I'm to report by the first of August."

I tried to make sense of what he said, but nothing fit. "But our wedding isn't until September. Surely they can change it."

"No, Elizabeth. They expect *me* to do the changing."

"I don't understand, Wynn. What are you saying?"

"I'm saying that there can't be a September wedding."

I felt the strength leave my body, but then my foggy brain began to work again. No September wedding. Wynn was to be at his posting in only two short weeks. I willed my strength back and began to think aloud about how we could accomplish the impossible.

"Oh, Elizabeth," Wynn said, "Would you—would you—?"

"I couldn't let you go without me, Wynn," I stammered. "The wedding might not be just as we planned, but it's the marriage that counts. And we will have our family and friends there, so it will still be beautiful." [22–25]

Every good gift and every perfect gift is from above,
and cometh down from the Father of lights,
with whom is no variableness, neither shadow of turning.
JAMES 1:17

EXAMPLE

I had often been held in my father's arms, but this time was different. We both sensed it. I was no longer his little girl. He brushed a kiss against my hair just above my ear and whispered to me. "I'm happy for you, Elizabeth. Happy—and sad—all at one time. Can you understand that?"

I nodded my head against his shoulder. Yes, I understood, for that was the way I felt. I hated to leave my family, but things had changed. I was not dependent on them anymore. I was cutting the ties and binding myself to another.

"I love you, Daddy," I said softly. "Thank you for everything. Thank you for raising me to be ready for a home of my own. I didn't realize it until now. But you did. You prepared me for this—for Wynn—and I thank you."

Suddenly I felt calm. Very calm and sure of myself. The arms of the man who held me made me think clearly of all that was ahead, and I suddenly realized that I was indeed ready for it. This was not just a whim, not just a schoolgirl romance. This was a deep and lasting love. I would be a wife and a helpmeet for the man I loved. My father had shown me how. Unconsciously, in all those years of my growing up, he had been showing me the way to a good marriage relationship—with his kindness, consideration, and strong loyalty to those he loved. I held him more tightly. I loved him very much. [30–31]

Be ye followers of me, even as I also am of Christ.
1 CORINTHIANS 11:1

CHOICES

I won't see you until tomorrow at the church," Wynn whispered. "Now don't go and change your mind."

"Not a chance," I assured him.

"I still can't believe it—tomorrow! And tomorrow is finally almost here. You'll never know what a fright it gave me when I got that early posting."

"Fright?"

"I thought I would have to leave you behind. I knew it would be unfair to ask you to wait for three or four or even five years. I was almost beside myself. I thought of quitting the Force, but I didn't have the money to start out someplace else. I never dreamed you would ever be able, and willing, to rush into a wedding like this. I hope you never feel that you've been cheated, Elizabeth."

"Cheated? Cheated out of what?"

"Out of the kind of wedding you've always dreamed of."

I laughed. "The fact is, Wynn, I spent very little time dreaming about weddings until I met you. *Then* I dreamed—I dreamed a lot. But the wedding wouldn't be much without you by my side, now would it? So, if there's a choice between the trimmings and you—then it's easy to leave out the trimmings."   [36–37]

Better is a dinner of herbs where love is,
than a stalled ox and hatred therewith.
PROVERBS 15:17

I must go," Wynn said after several moments. "My bride must be fresh and glowing on her wedding day; and if I don't let you sleep, it will be my fault if you aren't."

He saw me to the door and left. I went in to join the family. Father and Mother were ready to retire for the night. It had been a long, hard day for them. At Father's suggestion, we gathered in the living room for a time of Scripture reading and prayer. Tears squeezed from under our eyelids as we prayed together. Even Matthew, somewhat shyly, prayed aloud. I was touched at his earnest petition that God would bless his big sister Beth and her Wynn as they started out life together. It was a time I shall always remember. Never had I felt closer to my family than when we sat, hands intertwined, praying together as our tears flowed unheeded. [37]

Again I say unto you,
That if two of you shall agree on earth
as touching anything that they shall ask,
it shall be done for them of my Father
which is in heaven.
For where two or three are gathered together
in my name, there am I in the midst of them.
MATTHEW 18:19–20

GOD'S CHOICE

B eth," Julie whispered as we prepared for bed, "did you ever pray about the man you were to marry?"

"I prayed that I wouldn't make a wrong decision."

"And Mother prayed. She prays all the time. She doesn't say much about it, but I'm always finding her praying. And Father prays. In our family prayer time he always prays that God will guide each of his children in every decision of life."

"What are you getting at?" I asked.

"Maybe it was God who saw to it that you got together."

"I've always felt that," I answered simply.

"Well, I've never seen it that way before. Guess I sort of thought that God would pick out some serious older man with a kind, fatherly attitude—and poor looks. I'm not sure I was willing to trust Him to choose my future husband."

I laughed, but Julie was serious.

"No, Beth, I mean it. God didn't pick that kind of man for you. Wynn is just—is just—"

"Perfect," I finished for her.

"Perfect," she repeated with a sigh. "Do you think God could find me someone like that?"

"Oh, Julie. When God finds you the right one you won't think he is second to anyone." [40]

> *Delight thyself also in the Lord;*
> *and he shall give thee the desires of thine heart.*
> PSALM 37:4

THE BLESSING

Our wedding day was gloriously sunshiny. I stopped long enough to breathe a short prayer of thanks to God for arranging such a beautiful day. Then I turned my thoughts back to my wedding.

By the time Julie and I came downstairs, one carload had already left for the church. Mother and Father waited in the hall looking serene in spite of the last-minute flurries of the household. Mother's eyes misted as she looked at me.

We formed a close circle, the four of us—Father, Mother, Julie, and I—our arms intertwined as we stood together for one last time in the hallway of brother Jon's lovely Calgary home. Father led in prayer, asking that the Lord would make my home, wherever it might be, a place of love.

"Might there always be harmony and commitment, love and happiness. Might there be strength for the hard times, humor to ease the tense times, and shoulders always available for the times of tears," he prayed.

I found it difficult to keep the tears from falling, but I did not want to reach the church with swollen eyes and a smudged face, so I refused to allow myself to cry. Mother blew her nose softly and wiped at her eyes, and then we hastened to the car.

[46–47]

The Lord is nigh unto all them that call upon him,
to all that call upon him in truth.
PSALM 145:18

W hat will you remember about today, Elizabeth?" Wynn asked after we had settled into our train seats.

"The rush. And Father's prayer. He always prays with us before any big event. When Margaret was married, Father's prayer was so beautiful. I remember thinking, 'If I don't ever get married, I'll miss that.' Still, I wasn't convinced that the prayer was sufficient reason to risk a marriage."

"You're serious?"

"At the time I was. I didn't think I would ever feel inclined to marry."

"And I was taught to believe that every young girl is just waiting for the chance to lead some man to the altar."

"It wasn't that I was so against marriage. I just didn't like the insinuation that it was all a sensible girl thought about— that if I didn't marry, I was nothing. I didn't like that—that *bigotry*. Women are quite capable—"

"Hey, take it easy, Mrs. Delaney. You don't need to convince me. I'm sure that you could handle anything. But I'm glad you didn't decide you must prove your point for an entire lifetime. *You* might not need a man—but I need you. Your inner strength and your outer beauty, Elizabeth—I need both."   [51–52]

> *Who can find a virtuous woman?. . .*
> *She openeth her mouth with wisdom;*
> *and in her tongue is the law of kindness.*
> PROVERBS 31:10, 26

THE FUTURE

W e were both completely relaxed now. The long, beautiful, tiring, tense day was over. Our wedding had been lovely, but it now was in the past. Our whole future lay before us. Our marriage. I think that at that moment, as never before, I determined in my heart to make my marriage a thing even more beautiful than my wedding had been.

Perhaps Wynn felt it too, for he whispered softly against my hair, "This is just the beginning, Elizabeth. We have today as a memory, but we have all the tomorrows as exciting possibilities. We can shape them with hands of love to fulfill our fondest dreams. I wasn't much for marrying either, Elizabeth, but I am so glad you came into my life to change my mind. I've never been happier—and with God's help, I plan to make you happy, too." [53]

O satisfy us early with thy mercy;
that we may rejoice and be glad all our days.
And let the beauty of the Lord our God be upon us:
and establish thou the work of our hands upon us;
yea, the work of our hands establish thou it.
PSALM 90:14, 17

MISSION OF LOVE

I've never been so excited about heading north, Elizabeth," Wynn confided. "Always before I've known how much I was leaving behind. This time I can only think of what I am taking with me."

"I hope I never disappoint you, Wynn."

"I'm not worried about that. I only hope and pray that you are never disappointed. The North can be cruel, Elizabeth. It's beautiful, but it can be cruel, too. The people—they are simple, needy people—like children in many ways. I guess it's the people who draw me there. I love them in some mysterious way. They trust you, lean on you, so simply, so completely. You sort of feel you have to be worthy of their trust."

"And I'm sure you are."

"I don't know. It seems as if I've never been able to do enough. What they really need are doctors, schools, and most of all missions. Missions where they can really learn the truth about God and His plan for man. They have it all so mixed up in their thinking."

A new desire stirred within me, a desire not just to teach Wynn's people how to read and write, but how to find and worship God as well. Funny. I had never met them—not any of them—yet I felt as if I already loved them.   [75–76]

Thou shalt love thy neighbor as thyself.
MARK 12:31

WORLDLINESS

Edmonton was as far as the railroad went, so we traveled on a barge from there. The rains and wind started in the afternoon, and the barge offered no shelter from the cold and wetness. Because of the storm we stopped for the night at a trading post.

The shelter was only a shed filled with crates, barrels, and smelly hides. Charlie, an ill-kempt man, tended a stove in the middle of the room. The men from the barge greeted him boisterously, joking, swearing, and jabbing at one another.

Wynn fixed coffee and soup for everyone. Then he lifted me onto a pile of foulsmelling skins in the corner.

"I'm sorry, Elizabeth, but this will be your bed for tonight. Why don't you try to get some sleep?"

I wanted to retort, "Here?" But I knew that "here" was the best he could offer, so I simply nodded.

As the night progressed and bottles were emptied, the commotion grew. I nearly dozed once or twice. But then laughter or a stream of obscenity would jerk me awake again.

"Are you all right?" Wynn asked.

"I'm fine," I managed weakly, which I was, but I felt very out of place in a room with cursing, gambling men. It was the kind of thing I had avoided all my life.   [77–87]

Jesus . . . lifted up his eyes to heaven, and said, . . .
I pray not that thou shouldest take them out of the world,
but that thou shouldest keep them from the evil.
JOHN 17:1, 15

OPTIMISM

The barge hands, having been up all night, started the day in bad spirits. Now and then one of them would hold his head and weave back and forth. I wondered if they were in any condition to steer, especially when we hit some white water; but they seemed to be alert when they had to be. Wynn did not seem worried, so I relaxed. Eventually their dispositions improved. I even heard Blackjack singing later in the afternoon.

With the passing of the day, my disposition improved as well. Wynn had often been by my side to point out interesting items in the water or on the riverbanks. The sun was swinging to the west, the men were no longer cursing with every breath, and the country all around me seemed mysterious and exciting. Yes, things were definitely improved over yesterday.

Lying in that little cabin, I had wondered if I'd ever make it as a Mountie's wife. Today I was confident I could. We would soon be at the post, and Wynn had said we would have good accommodations there. I wasn't sure how many nights it would take us to make the trip, but I was now certain I could endure. I had gotten through the first night, and it surely couldn't be any worse. From here on I would have no problem. [92]

The Lord is my strength and my shield;
my heart trusted in him, and I am helped:
therefore my heart greatly rejoiceth;
and with my song will I praise him.
PSALM 28:7

PESTS

My optimism was short-lived. Although our accommodations were much better, giant mosquitoes attacked me all night. I rose tired and grumpy.

"Mosquitoes are one of the area's worst pests," Wynn informed me as the annoying insects swarmed around us. "Blackflies are another real plague to man and beast alike."

Wynn was right. The mosquitoes were joined that day by the blackflies. I thought I would be chewed to pieces. Right before my eyes, new welts would rise on my arms. I hated to think what my face must look like. I was almost frantic with the itching.

Wynn was sympathetic. "I might have something that will help," he offered and went to dig around in his medical supplies.

He came back with an ointment. It had a vile smell and looked awful, but I allowed him to rub it on anyway. It helped some, but it didn't discourage the dreadful insects from taking more bites out of me.

"Why didn't they bother us yesterday?" I asked.

"The wind and the rain kept them away. They can't fly well in wind, and they don't care for the rain either."

"Really?" I was ready to pray for more wind and rain. Anything to be rid of the miserable pests. [94]

Surely he shall deliver thee from the snare of the fowler,
and from the noisome pestilence.
PSALM 91:3

SURVIVAL

Alone the next night in a trapper's cozy cabin, Wynn and I spread a worn woolen blanket in front of the fire and settled down to talk. Suddenly a strange, mournful, bloodcurdling sound interrupted us. I had gotten used to the coyote's cry, but this was something entirely different. I pressed closer to Wynn.

"A timber wolf," Wynn offered. "But there's nothing to worry about. Listen carefully. You can almost count how many there are in the pack by the difference in their cries. They are a part of our world here—a part that needs to be respected but not feared. Accept them—maybe even enjoy them if you can."

The wolves were a part of Wynn's wilderness, and his calm acceptance helped me see the wild creatures in another light.

Another howl. Another shiver. Another explanation from Wynn. He pictured the pack around us, locating and identifying each member. He described them as needy, hungry creatures that depended on nature and their skills to feed themselves and their families.

"Contrary to what you may have heard, wolves hunt only to survive. In the wilderness, survival is not always easy."

I listened to the echoing calls of the wolves as they moved away from the cabin. My heart quit thumping. I found myself even wishing them good hunting. [96–99]

I know all the fowls of the mountains:
and the wild beasts of the field are mine.
PSALM 50:11

SUBSTITUTES

We took the trail the next morning to the small, hastily constructed buildings that formed the small outpost. When we reached the fort, I looked about at the sorry arrangement of small buildings. Even from the outside, I was sure I wouldn't have wanted to stay overnight in any of them. I was so glad Wynn had arranged for the cabin.

"I think you should wait out here," Wynn said to me. I wondered why, but did not question him. I found a nearby tree stump and sat down.

Wynn was not in the cabin for long. He returned with a look of frustration on his face.

"What's wrong? Are they drunk?"

"Drunk isn't the word for it. They are *out*! Every last one of them. I couldn't even raise them. I don't like their drinking, but I can't stop them. That's their business—their way of life— their way of easing through the difficulties of life in the North. When men don't have God, they need substitutes. To my way of thinking, whiskey is a poor substitute—but many men depend on it." [100–101]

If we have forgotten the name of our God,
or stretched out our hands to a strange god;
shall not God search this out?
for he knoweth the secrets of the heart.
PSALM 44:20–21

WANDERING

At best, the road could be described as a trail. It wound up and down, around and through, following the path of least resistance, much like a river would do. The horses strained up steep hills, then slid their way to the bottom again, the wagon jolting behind. At one point the trail went nearly straight down. Fearing for our safety, Wynn asked me to walk down the incline. I held my breath as he drove the wagon, brakes locked, down the hill, always on the heels of the sliding horses.

When Wynn reached the bottom, I hurried to meet him. His warning to slow down came too late. My body was already moving far too fast for my clumsy feet. I felt myself rolling end over end.

"Elizabeth, are you all right?" Wynn gasped, his face white.

I struggled to clear my head and regain my composure while Wynn checked me for injuries. Thankfully, I had no more damage than scratches and bruises.

Convinced that I was all right, Wynn turned his attention to the team. Oblivious to the commotion, they had plodded on without us. Wynn caught the team about a quarter of a mile down the road. They had not exactly followed the trail, though, and Wynn was hard put to back them out of the dead end they had led themselves into among the trees.   [102–104]

> *With my whole heart have I sought thee:*
> *O let me not wander from thy commandments.*
> PSALM 119:10

RECEIVING

As we approached the cabin, I looked down in dismay at my bites, scratches, and bruises, realizing that I would have to meet strangers in such a disgraceful condition. I relaxed a bit when I saw that the woman who welcomed us into the one-room, two-family home was just as mosquito-bitten as I.

With great ceremony, almost as if they had been expecting us, the couples seated us at their crude table. The woman at the stove brought huge bowls of steaming stew and set them before us. I wanted to protest when I realized that the women were giving up their places at the table, but Wynn nudged me, and I understood that to decline their invitation might offend them. I smiled appreciatively. The food smelled delicious.

I recognized none of the vegetables I saw in my dish. Wynn informed me that the women were experts at combing the forest for edible plants. I smiled at them again, thanking them for sharing their supper.

"We be so glad to see ya, yer doin' *us* the favor," declared the older one with simple courtesy. [107–108]

And while he was at Bethany . . . as he sat at the table,
a woman came with an alabaster flask
of ointment of pure nard, very costly,
and she broke the flask
and poured it over his head.
MARK 14:3

HOME

The last leg of our journey was quiet. I felt too excited to talk. My mind was full of questions. *What will our cabin be like? What will our neighbors be like? Will there be any white women at the Post? Will the Indians like me and accept me?*

Finally Wynn spoke. "If I've got it worked out right, the settlement should be right over this next hill."

In my excitement I reached over and gave him a quick hug which sent his stetson tumbling into the dust. By the time Wynn got my arms untangled and the team stopped, his Royal North West Mounted Police hat had been run over by the heavy wagon wheel. Wynn walked back to retrieve the flattened hat, and I was relieved when he returned smiling. After punching it here and there, he settled it back on his head. Except for a few unsightly lumps, it was in better shape than I had dared to hope.

Wynn was right. When we rounded the brow of the hill before us, the little settlement lay at our feet. I restrained myself from hugging Wynn again. Instead, he hugged me.

"There it is, Elizabeth," he whispered against my cheek. "There's home." [112–113]

> *For we know that if our earthly house*
> *of this tabernacle were dissolved,*
> *we have a building of God,*
> *an house not made with hands,*
> *eternal in the heavens.*
> 2 CORINTHIANS 5:1

A large flock of birds chattered in nearby trees, no doubt making plans to return to lands where winter snow would not blow. From the village, a quarter of a mile from our cabin, I could hear voices and barking dogs. I breathed deeply of the morning air. The hillsides were covered with evergreens and scattered with poplar and birch trees.

It was beautiful country. I would make it. I would! I would fix the house, clean myself up, and prove to Wynn that I could be happy here—as long as he was with me. A nagging fear gripped me then. What about all the times when Wynn's duties would take him elsewhere? Like last night when he had to care for the borrowed team? Wynn had done only what needed to be done. I tried to convince myself that it was silly to let one disappointment ruin the excitement of starting our new life together. It was going to take a lot of resolve for me to create a home, a happy home, in Wynn's wilderness. I couldn't crumble like I had last night every time I faced difficulties. I wanted to be happy here. Most of all, I wanted to make Wynn happy. I was going to need help. I knew of only one true source readily available to me. I stopped for a few moments of prayer.

[122–123]

The Lord preserveth the faithful,
and plentifully rewardeth the proud doer.
Be of good courage, and he shall strengthen your heart. . .
PSALM 31:23–24

SATISFACTION

By the time Wynn arrived home that afternoon, the house was in quite good order. The large room, which was to be Wynn's office, still needed to be arranged, but Wynn had told me to leave that to him.

Our supper that night came from tins of North West Mounted Police rations. I had no other meat and no vegetables of any kind. It was a simple meal, but we ate with a deep feeling of satisfaction. We were where we belonged, doing what we felt called to do. We had a home, and we had one another. There was much to be done before we would be settled, but we had made a good start. I forgot my tired arms and back and chatted with Wynn about all the possibilities the little cabin held. I looked out of my window to the rough little shanty with its crooked door and crude shingles and felt more thankful for it than for the fanciest bathroom.

"Thanks, Wynn, for having that little building built so soon. I appreciate your thoughtfulness."

"I want to make you as happy and as comfortable as possible," he said with a smile.

This was our start in our new life. After a good, hot soak I was sure that I would feel content with my world.   [126]

Give to every man that asketh of thee; . . .
And as ye would that men should do to you,
do ye also to them likewise.
LUKE 6:30–31

FRIENDLINESS

Our little house looks much different since you've fixed it up, and I'm proud of you." Wynn's smile of appreciation filled me with a warm glow. "I've been wondering, though, if you might find time to get acquainted with some of our neighbors. It would be nice if you could find some friends."

"I've been meaning to. Every day I plan to walk over to the store and meet some of the people, but I keep finding more things that need to be done, so I keep putting it off. I'll have some time this week, though. Tomorrow I need to do the washing, but maybe Tuesday I can go."

"I'd like that. I'd like you to get to know some of the women so you might have company on the days I'm away."

"But how can I get to know people when I can't talk to them?" I asked, finally revealing to Wynn my real reason for not going to the village.

"You'll be able to talk to them," he assured me. "It will be hard, and there will be times when you'll have problems expressing yourself. But you will pick up a few of their words quickly. And many of the Indians already know a number of English words, and they are very good at making themselves understood by using their limited English and their hands. You'll catch on quickly—but you can't learn about them if you are not with them." [128–129]

A man that hath friends must shew himself friendly.
PROVERBS 18:24

BALANCING ACCOUNTS

Wynn began to laugh. He lifted my chin and kissed me on the nose, but laughter was still in his eyes. I realized I had just revealed my city breeding, and Wynn was laughing at my ignorance of the ways of the wilderness. I could either get angry with him for laughing at me or choose to laugh with him. For a moment I was tempted to be angry, but then I remembered my father's prayer—the part about humor for the difficult times—and I began to laugh. Well, at least I smiled. "I take it I'm offtrack?"

Wynn smiled and kissed my nose again. "A little. It's true that it's a trading post and that trappers bring their furs there. But Mr. McLain is very happy to accept cash as well. But even that isn't necessary. We have a charge account there. You pick what you need, and Mr. McLain will enter it in his little book under my name. I also would like you to keep an account of what you spend, so I can enter it in my book. Then, when the end of the month comes, McLain and I compare our records, balance our accounts, and I pay what I owe him. [131–132]

We'll do better at keeping
our earthly accounts balanced
if we keep in mind that one day
we will have to account to God.
Every one of us shall give account of himself to God.
ROMANS 14:12

ADJUSTMENTS

Why hadn't Wynn warned me that Mr. McLain's wife was Indian? Or had he known? And why hadn't I prepared myself for the possibility? I had so much wanted to have one white woman in the area. I felt an intense disappointment. There wasn't a woman in the whole area with whom I could share intimacies, who would understand women's fashions and women's fears. It was going to be a lonely time, the years ahead. They would be sure to get me down if I didn't take some serious steps to avoid allowing myself to be caught in the trap of self-pity. But before I could do anything, I needed to sort out my thoughts and to spend some time in prayer.

I did pray as soon as I got home, and I was soon feeling much better. As I ironed, I thought about what I might have to offer the Indian women, about what we as wives had in common, and about what I could do to improve their living conditions. I began to feel excited about the prospects. By the time the ironing was completed, my plans had begun to take shape.   [136–137]

Let every one of us please his neighbor
for his good to edification.
ROMANS 15:2

INVITATION

Come?"

The invitation caught me off-guard, but I responded quickly.

"Yes, I'd love to come." We followed the path to the stream, the stream to the river, and then followed the trail that paralleled the river. Then we headed through the bush and walked for about another mile before we came to the berry patch. The women talked excitedly as they pointed at the bushes thick with berries. Then they set to work. I couldn't begin to keep up with them. Their hands flashed. I tried to follow their examples but I spilled more berries than I got into my pail, so I decided to take my time and get the berries where they belonged.

Near noon, the youngest came over to where I was picking. She looked in my pail and seemed to show approval. Then she showed me her basket. She had picked twice as many. She quickly picked a few handfuls and threw them into my pail. The others came with their full containers, gathered around me, and they too began to pick berries and deposit them in my pail. With four of us picking, the pail was full in no time. I thanked them with a smile, and we all got up and stretched to ease the ache in our backs.

Then we started home. I could hardly wait to tell Wynn about my adventure with these generous Indian women.

[140–141]

Two are better than one;
for they have a good reward for their labour.
ECCLESIASTES 4:9

SUPERIORITY

When we reached my cabin, I smiled and stepped back, nodding them a good-day after my attempts at verbal communication had failed. They smiled in return and started down the path. Anna was the last to turn and go. As she passed me, she stopped, leaned forward, pointed at Evening Star, and whispered, "She doesn't understand English talk." Then she followed the others down the path. I stared after her with my mouth open.

We went for berries the following day too. Anna was there again, so I directed my inquiries to her, determined that I would not be cheated out of conversation again. I learned that she and Mrs. Sam were both married to white trappers and that Anna spoke English well because she had attended a mission school in another area. Beaver River had no school. I found out later that she had had more schooling than her trapper husband, even though it was only the equivalent of about grade four. She was the one who did the figuring when she and her husband went to the trading post.

I grew to admire Anna. Despite her education and ability to speak English, she did not consider herself superior to any of the others, just different from them. [143–145]

Every one that exalteth himself shall be abased;
and he that humbleth himself shall be exalted.
LUKE 18:14

BITTERNESS

Another white woman lived in the village after all—McLain's sister. I rapped gently on her door, eager to get acquainted. I knocked louder after getting no response. "Come," a voice finally called. I entered timidly.

Seated in a corner, staring at the blank wall, her hands folded in her lap, was Miss McLain. "You're the lawman's wife," she stated in a raspy voice. "What do you want?"

"Well, I—I just heard that a white woman lived here, and I wanted to meet you."

"White woman?" she said with contempt. "This is no place for a white woman. Why did you come here?"

After I answered, she let me know that I had done something incredibly wrong or stupid, perhaps both. I felt condemned, but I also felt challenged. "And why did *you* come here?" I asked.

"I came," she said deliberately, hissing out each word, "because there was nowhere else I could go."

"I'm—I'm sorry," was all I could manage to say. Finally I was able to add, "I think I'd better go."

I was glad to step into the warm sunshine and close the door on the angry woman inside. What deep bitterness drove her? Surely it would destroy her if something wasn't done. But as for me, I hoped I would never again encounter her.   [154–156]

Let all bitterness, and wrath, and anger, and clamour,
and evil speaking, be put away from you, with all malice.
EPHESIANS 4:31

COMPASSION

As I left Miss McLain's, Mrs. McLain called pleasantly, "Mrs. Delaney, could you join me for tea?"

I wanted to head for the security of my home, but that would have been rude. I smiled instead and said, "That is most kind. Thank you."

She led me into a pleasant room, a combination of white and Indian worlds. After seating me, she went to her kitchen and returned with tea and slices of blueberry loaf cake.

"So, are you feeling settled in Beaver River?" she asked.

"Oh, yes. Quite settled."

We went on with small talk for many moments, and then she became more personal. Eventually it dawned on me that this was the kind of conversation I had been aching to have— the kind for which I had been seeking white companionship.

As I was about to leave, she spoke softly. "Don't judge poor Katherine too quickly," she said. "There is much sorrow and hurt in her past. Maybe with love and understanding—" She stopped and sighed. "And time," she added. "Maybe with time she will overcome it."

I looked at her with wonder but asked no questions. I nodded, thanked her again, and hurried home. [156–160]

Finally, be ye all of one mind,
having compassion one of another,
love as brethren, be pitiful, be courteous.
1 PETER 3:8

HATE

I stood in awe as Nimmie continued. I had never heard the story of David and Goliath told in this fashion. Where had she heard it? And why was she telling it to the children in English? Few of them could understand all of the English words, yet not one of them was moving.

I was puzzled but I was also intrigued. How often did Nimmie tell the children stories, and how often were they from the Bible? Did she always interpret the stories with Indian concepts?

"I love the Bible stories," Nimmie explained without being asked. "I like the stories about Jesus best."

"You know, Nimmie, all those things really happened."

"They are all true?" Nimmie asked incredulously. "And those wicked people really did kill Him—for no reason? That's hateful. Only a white man could do such a thing."

"But he didn't stay dead, you know. I'd be happy to study the story with you if you'd like."

"I'd like that." She paused, then added, "Elizabeth, I'm sorry about what I said concerning the white man. Sometimes I just cannot understand the way men gnash and tear at one another— it's worse than animals." [168–171]

> *Love your enemies, bless them that curse you,*
> *do good to them that hate you,*
> *and pray for them which despitefully use you, . . .*
> *That ye may be the children of your Father which is in heaven.*
> MATTHEW 5:44–45

TEAM WORK

Wynn's sled dogs had been carefully picked by the men of the Force who had preceded him. They had been chosen for their endurance, dependability, and strength, but not particularly for their good dispositions. Many of them were scrappers. For that reason they had to be tied well out of range of one another. Harnessing them to the sleigh was a tough job. Things could be going well and suddenly one of the dogs would get mad at another one and a fight would break out. Before long the whole team would be in a scrap, tangling the harness and making a general mess of things.

Wynn had been talking about choosing his own dog team and training them himself. With different training, he thought the dogs might be better tempered and make less problems on the trail. It would take time and work, but it sounded like a good idea to me. I didn't care much for Wynn's dogs, but the team was very necessary. Wynn used his dogs almost every day during the winter. His team was considered to be one of the fastest in the area, and speed was important to a policeman. A few minutes might mean the difference between life or death. But Wynn had learned to appreciate something more important than the speed of his sled dogs. While on the trail they laid aside all grudges and pulled together.   [178–179]

Keep the unity of the Spirit in the bond of peace.
EPHESIANS 4:3

SUFFERING

Little by little I learned Katherine McLain's story and found out why she was so deeply bitter and troubled. Orphaned at age three, Katherine was raised, along with her brother Ian, by a kind but poor family in the East. The children had been allowed to attend the local school as high as the grades went, but when they reached their teens they were on their own. Katherine became a schoolteacher and eventually fell in love, but her fiancé called off the wedding because of untrue accusations made by his sister about Katherine.

Katherine had never buried her bitterness. In her twenty years in the North, she had nursed it and fostered it and held it to her until now it was a terrible, deep festering wound in her soul. She was miserable; she deserved to be miserable; she seemed to enjoy being miserable; and she did a wonderful job of making those around her miserable too.

In spite of her bitterness and anger, however, I began to like Miss McLain. I felt both sorry for her and angry with her. Others had suffered; others had been treated unfairly. But they had lived through it. Surely she could pull herself out of her misery if she had a mind to.   [189–190]

> *The sufferings of this present time*
> *are not worthy to be compared*
> *with the glory which shall be revealed in us.*
> ROMANS 8:18

CONSCIENCE

One stormy morning Wynn announced that he had to take a trip south. He made sure I had plenty of wood, told me not to go out until the storm was over, kissed me goodbye, and left.

Wynn did not return that night nor the next, but the storm did not let up until the third day. I wanted to break out of my confining cabin and find human companionship. But first I had to restart the fire. I went to get the wood stacked outside the door, but the door would not budge. A snow drift had it blocked. I spent the day wrapped in blankets and a heavy fur rug, but even they did not keep out the cold. That night I let Kip, the husky we had chosen as a pet, sleep on my feet.

I awoke to the sound of digging. Mr. McLain had noticed that no smoke was coming from my chimney and had come to check on me. I learned from him that the storm had been tough on everyone. Nimmie had a whole fort full of people that she was trying to get hot food into. A number of the families had run out of wood. A little girl and a few older people had died.

I knew that Nimmie needed my help. I was torn between going to her and waiting in the cabin in case Wynn came home. My conscience finally won over my heart, and I reached for my heavy coat.

[195–201]

> *I was an hungered, and ye gave me meat:*
> *I was thirsty, and ye gave me drink: . . .*
> *I was sick, and ye visited me.*
> MATTHEW 25:35–36

OVERPROTECTION

We shut the door on the whining Kip and made our way across the drifts.

"You won't be able to keep him away from other dogs forever," Mr. McLain said. "He's smart and he's strong. Appears to me that he could handle himself fine against another dog."

"Are you saying—?"

"I'm saying that, with a child or a dog, you've got to give them a chance to grow up—natural like. You can't pamper them forever, or you spoil them. They can never be what they were meant to be. Kip's a Husky. Sure, they are a scrappy bunch when the need arises. And the need will arise someday. Here in the North, it's bound to. I think you oughta give Kip the chance to prove himself before he gets up against an animal when his life depends upon his fighting skill."

I wanted to argue—to tell him that Kip would never need to fight, that I would keep him away from such circumstances. But I knew Mr. McLain was probably right. Kip was a northern dog. He would have to be prepared to live in the North. I hated the thought, but it was true. [201–202]

God does not always keep us from adversity,
but He strengthens us through it.
My grace is sufficient for thee:
for my strength is made perfect in weakness.
2 CORINTHIANS 12:9

TEMPER

The situation at the store was even worse than I had expected. People were crowded in everywhere. Nimmie was busily serving hot soup, but she soon ran out of bowls.

I went to see if Miss McLain had some we could use. I found her sitting before her fireplace. I looked at her in bewilderment, wondering if she was totally oblivious to all that was going on next door. Struggling to control my anger at her indifference, I gathered the dishes she said we could use and turned to go.

"Just make sure they're boiled when you're done with them," she stated, her eyes not leaving the fire.

I swung around to face her. "Do you realize that people just beyond that wall are fighting for their lives? And that Nimmie has been up half the night taking care of them? And here you sit, all bundled up in your self-pity. Well, I think you were well rid of the man. If he would desert you because of a whining, accusing sister, he wasn't much of a man. And anyone who would nurse a twenty-year-old hurt while people in the next room are suffering isn't much of a woman either."

When I realized what I had done, the tears started to flow. I had prayed so diligently for this woman. I had tried so hard to show her love and compassion. Now, in a moment of anger, I had wiped out any faint possibilities of progress.   [203–205]

Let every man be swift to hear, slow to speak, slow to wrath.
For the wrath of man worketh not the righteousness of God.
JAMES 1:19–20

Nimmie had just finished checking a swollen hand when I heard her exclaim, "Katherine! Are you all right? Do you want something?"

"Yes. I want to help."

I don't know who was more astounded—Nimmie or I. We both looked at Miss McLain with our mouths open. Her eyes were red and swollen, and I could tell she had been weeping.

"I want to help," she repeated. "Would you tell me what I can do?"

"Well, we'll need the dishes. We haven't had time to wash the dishes yet."

Without a word, Miss McLain moved to the dishpan, rolled up her sleeves, and set to work.

After that, Miss McLain never missed coming to Bible study with Nimmie. Though she was still difficult at times, her attitude had changed from the inside out. I never did apologize—not that I wasn't willing to do so. It just didn't seem appropriate under the circumstances. Instead, I just thanked the Lord for turning something bad into something good.　　　　[206–210]

Depart from evil, and do good; seek peace, and pursue it. . . .
The Lord is nigh unto them that are of a broken heart;
and saveth such as be of a contrite spirit.
PSALM 34:14, 18

WAIT

In the dead of night we were awakened by someone calling Wynn's name. Both of us sat bolt upright in bed. Then Wynn reached for his clothes and hurried into them.

I listened to the anxious voices coming from the other room. Soon Wynn was back. "It's Evening Star," he said. "She's having trouble delivering her baby. I'll be back as soon as I can."

I got out of bed, put more wood on the fire, and picked up my Bible. I paged through the Psalms, but I couldn't concentrate on my reading. Finally I closed my eyes and began to pray. For Evening Star and the unborn little one. For Wynn, that he would have wisdom. For myself, that God would enable me to concentrate on His Word.

After some minutes, I went back to the Bible. Again my eyes skimmed the pages. My spirit was calm now. My trembling had ceased. I read passage after passage until I came to Psalm 27:14: "Wait on the Lord: be of good courage, and he shall strengthen thine heart; wait, I say, on the Lord."

"Yes, Lord," I prayed. "All I can do is wait." I picked up the sweater I was knitting for the new baby and worked while I waited. [212-213]

Someday our Lord will return,
and He wants us to work while we await Him.
Therefore be ye also ready: for in such an hour
as ye think not the Son of man cometh.
MATTHEW 24:44

THE LAW

I came home from Crazy Mary's feeling sick. Surely there was some other way to deal with the situation.

"Elizabeth," Wynn responded to my pleading, "if I let Mary go, none of the people will have respect for the law. Besides, Crazy Mary would try it again. She has an inner drive to accumulate pelts, and she will stop at nothing to get them. But she will get a fair trial," Wynn assured me. "They will take into consideration her mental state. And she will be better cared for there than she would be out on her own on the trapline."

Sadness filled Wynn's eyes. To lock Mary up, even with tender care, would not be good for her. She needed freedom.

"There is another thing to think about, Elizabeth," Wynn added. "If I don't handle this properly and carry out the demands of the law, Smith or someone else will handle it in his own way, according to his own laws, and Mary could be killed or beaten. I was sent up north to uphold the law, Elizabeth. To the best of my ability, I intend to do just that, God helping me."

I knew there was no need to discuss it further. Wynn would follow the dictates of the law, not his own feelings. [220–221]

Submit yourselves to every ordinance of man
for the Lord's sake . . . as unto them
that are sent by him for the punishment of evildoers,
and for the praise of them that do well.
1 PETER 2:13–15

PREJUDICE

Each time Nimmie and I met together for our Bible study, she taught me some lesson. She was a patient, beautiful person with a heart of love and an open mind to truth.

I talked to Wynn about her one night as we were stretched out before our open fire.

"I've learned to love Nimmie," I said. "She's a beautiful person. It's strange—when I first saw her I was so disappointed. I didn't tell you that before, did I?"

Wynn shook his head, his eyes studying mine.

"I guess I didn't tell you because I was ashamed of myself. I was prejudiced, you know. I didn't realize it, but I was. I love the Indian people, but I had wanted someone to share things with. And I—I thought—that—well that—the person needed to be like me—white. Well, I was wrong. I was wanting a white woman, and instead I found a friend, a very special friend, in Nimmie.

Wynn reached out to take my hand. I think he understood what I was trying to say. [222-223]

But if ye have respect to persons, ye commit sin.
JAMES 2:9

FAITH

One day Nimmie came to see me alone. "I've been thinking about that verse we studied yesterday," she started, "the one about Christ dying for the ungodly. Well, I'm ungodly."

"Yes, we all are without God," I agreed in a near whisper.

Nimmie's eyes flew open. "You too?"

"Yes. Me too. The Bible says, 'All have sinned,' remember?"

"I remember. I guess I just didn't think of it."

"Nimmie, when I realized that I could do nothing to atone for my sins, I did the only thing one can do. I accepted what God has provided for all—His forgiveness. Jesus died for our sins so that we need not die for our own. I don't understand that kind of love, but I know it's real, for I have felt it. When I took His Son as my Savior, that love filled my whole person. Where I had misery and fear before, now I have peace and joy."

"And He would do that for me?"

"He wants to. That's why He came. He loves you, Nimmie."

We bowed our heads. I prayed, and then Nimmie prayed— a beautiful, simple prayer of faith, repentance, joy, and praise. When Nimmie left that day she was more than a special friend; she was a beloved sister as well. [223–225]

If we confess our sins,
he is faithful and just to forgive us our sins,
and to cleanse us from all unrighteousness.
1 JOHN 1:9

PROVISION

After fire destroyed the Hudson's Bay Store, Wynn called a meeting of all the people. The Indians relied heavily on the trading post and did not store food ahead except for roots, herbs, and dried berries. By this time of year, even those were in short supply. Our future looked bleak indeed. Wynn stood before the Indians and spoke in their language. Nimmie whispered the translation to me.

"We meet together because we are one. We must care for one another. We have lost the trading post and the food it supplied. Now we must find our own way. It is not a new way. It has been done for many moons by our fathers. But it is a hard way. It will take us all working together.

"We have the forests and the streams. They will not forsake us. They have meat for the taking. We will hunt together and share what we find. We have plants we can gather from under the snow. You know them well. We will send out groups to gather them. And, most importantly, we have a God who sees us and knows that we are in need. He has promised to care for His children."

When Wynn finished speaking, the people filed away silently. But the look of despair upon their faces had been replaced with a glimmer of hope. [235–236]

But my God shall supply all your need
according to his riches in glory by Christ Jesus.
PHILIPPIANS 4:19

GIFTS OF LOVE

The McLains decided to take the long journey back to the city to get supplies to rebuild the trading post. They had very little to take. They had no clothing and no provisions except what they were given. Wynn made sure they had a good rifle and some shells. As the McLains prepared for travel, villagers came shyly forward and offered love gifts of food or clothing or traps. I knew that the people desperately needed the things they were giving away, yet so did the McLains. The gifts were given in love, and the McLains accepted them in love.

At the last minute, Nimmie drew me aside. "I have a wonderful secret," she said. "I am going to have a baby. Just think— after ten years of marriage, I am going to have a baby!"

"Oh, Nimmie," was all I could say, and I took her in my arms and cried all over her fur parka.

I prayed that they would arrive safely. And I prayed with all my heart that things would go well for Nimmie and that God would protect her unborn child. [238–239]

And there came a certain poor widow,
and she threw in two mites, . . .
This poor widow hath cast more in,
than all they which have cast into the treasury:
For all they did cast in of their abundance;
but she of her want did cast in all that she had.
MARK 12:42–44

BEAUTY

Wynn and I walked over the crunching snow in the moonlight. From the cabins surrounding the little clearing, soft light flickered on the billowy banks of snow.

"It's pretty, isn't it?" I said to Wynn.

"I think so, but I thought you wanted the snow to go."

"I do, but I really don't mind the snow itself—it's pretty, and I have enjoyed it—walking in it, looking at it. It's the wind I hate. I can't stand the wind. It sends chills all through me. It seems so vengeful somehow. I hate it!"

Wynn reached over to take my hand as we walked.

"I wish you could learn to appreciate the wind, Elizabeth. God made the wind too. It has many purposes, and you will never be at peace here until you have made friends with the wind. Try to understand it—to find beauty in it."

He pulled me to a stop. "Look. See that snowbank? Notice the way the top peaks and drops over in a curve—the velvet softness of the purple shadow created by the glow of the moon. See how beautiful it is."

He pointed out other wind sculptures around the clearing.

I laughed. "All right," I assured him. "I will try to find beauty in the wind." [242–243]

The heavens declare the glory of God;
and the firmament sheweth his handiwork.
PSALM 19:1

HOPE

T his winter has been hard for you, hasn't it?"

"It's been hard for everyone," I answered.

"But the rest—they are used to the hardships. You haven't been. Has it—has it been too much?"

"I admit I will be very glad for a fresh carrot and a piece of cake. I will even admit that spinach, which I hate, might taste good. But I am not sorry that I came with you, Wynn."

"I'm glad to hear you say that, Elizabeth. I have something to say too. Something I maybe should have said long ago, but I want to say now, with all my heart—with all my love. I'm proud of you, Elizabeth. Proud of your strength, your support, your ability to adjust to hard things. You've been my help, my support, my right arm, Elizabeth. I don't know what I ever would have done without you. You've more than proved me wrong—over and over. You belong here—with me."

Wynn kissed me, and I brushed away tears of happiness.

Then I heard the grinding of the wagon wheels. They were coming. Just over the hill was Nimmie. Just over the hill were the needed supplies—and hope. I gave Wynn one more kiss with all my love wrapped up in it, and I turned to meet the oncoming wagon. Spring had come. [254–255]

O clap your hands, all ye people;
shout unto God with the voice of triumph.
PSALM 47:1

WHEN BREAKS

THE DAWN

PREFERENCES

If only I had something special to celebrate this great occasion—the safe return of our friends, the coming of the food supply. But I had nothing. I made some simple biscuits, nearly using up the last of the flour. I had no shortening except rendered bear tallow. I did not enjoy the taste of it, but the biscuits would be as hard as rocks without it.

We gathered around our small table, and Wynn led us in prayer. His voice broke as he expressed his gratitude to our heavenly Father for getting the wagons to the settlement in time to prevent any real hardship. I was reminded again of the heavy responsibility Wynn had carried over the past months.

We enjoyed our simple meal together. Nimmie exclaimed over the biscuits. "Bear tallow, isn't it? I've really missed it—it tastes so good."

I laughed. I guess preferences have a lot to do with background.

"Did you hate to come back?" I asked Nimmie later.

She spoke slowly, guardedly. "I loved seeing your world. But as the days and weeks went by, I was so homesick for the rivers, the forests, I could hardly wait to come home." [20–25]

Just as we all have individual preferences,
we also have individual gifts.

There are diversities of gifts, but the same Spirit.
1 CORINTHIANS 12:5

EXPECTANCY

Nimmie and I planted our gardens with seeds she had brought back. I could hardly wait for the tender plants to appear. Nimmie was far more patient than I.

She was also more patient about her impending delivery, which was drawing near. She didn't seem to feel anything other than anticipation, but for some reason I felt alarm.

What if something were to go wrong? What will we do if we need a doctor? For the first time I began to feel just a little thankful that I wasn't the one waiting for the arrival of a baby. I had not shared my prayers with Wynn, but for some weeks I had been praying nightly that God would grant my desire for a family— and soon. We had already been married for almost a year and it seemed as if God should be answering my prayer by now.

Still, as I looked at Nimmie, daily becoming larger and heavier, I felt the shiver of fear run through me, and I thought more and more about her impending delivery time. I prayed more earnestly for her and the baby than I had ever prayed for anything in my entire life.

"Please, dear God," I pleaded daily, almost hourly, "please let everything be all right." [50]

My soul, wait thou only upon God;
for my expectation is from him.
PSALM 62:5

DESIRES

As a surprise for me on our first anniversary, Wynn planned a camping trip. We walked most of the morning and came to a lovely spot beside a small pond made by beavers damming the stream. The fir trees, thick about us, made a canopy over our heads.

"Here is where we stop," said Wynn, much to my delight.

After our evening meal, we sat with our backs against a fallen log and watched a beaver couple work. With our fingers intertwined, we talked softly about our inner dreams and plans for the future.

I learned much about my husband on that camping trip. I had thought I already knew him well, but he shared with me so many new things—about his childhood, about his training, about his desires and goals.

I think he guessed part of my desires when I spoke about Nimmie and her coming baby with such wistfulness.

"You'd like a child, wouldn't you, Elizabeth?"

"Oh, so much," I told him. "I can hardly wait. And here we have been married for a whole year and . . ." I did not finish the sentence for fear that Wynn would somehow think I was blaming him. "God knows when the time is right," I finished instead.

Wynn nodded, and we talked of other things.   [58–59]

Thou openest thine hand,
and satisfiest the desire of every living thing.
PSALM 145:16

124

WONDER

I stood for many minutes looking down at Nimmie's tiny new baby girl. Her dainty curled fists lay in a relaxed position on her chubby cheeks, her dark hair slightly curled over her forehead. Her eyes were closed, and just a trace of eyelash showed because of the slight puffiness due to her recent arrival.

"A little herb-gatherer," I said with tears in my eyes. "Oh, Nimmie, she's beautiful!"

There may be those who would have argued with me. A newborn is really not too beautiful. But she was healthy and whole, and given a few days to adjust to her new world, I knew she would look beautiful. I felt a twinge within me again— something which told me that just at this moment, Nimmie was one of the most blessed people I knew.

As I looked at the tiny, beautiful baby in Nimmie's arms, a prayer arose in my heart. She was here, and she was safe, and she was about the prettiest thing I had ever seen.   [64–65]

For thou has possessed my reins:
thou hast covered me in my mother's womb.
I will praise thee;
for I am fearfully and wonderfully made.
PSALM 139:13–14

KNOWLEDGE

Nimmie returned from the main village with good news. The chief had said we could start a school as long as we didn't interfere with the children's rightful duties.

My mind could hardly work in the excitement. Another of my prayers had been answered. We would get our school.

At last the long-awaited day arrived. I took a deep breath and smiled at Nimmie, giving her the nod to "ring our bell."

The minutes ticked by, and no one showed up. "They'll come," Nimmie assured me, unperturbed.

Nimmie was right. The children came a few at a time until the schoolhouse was crowded. I was exhilarated! *Wait till I tell Wynn!* I exulted. I remembered his words of caution: *Don't be too disappointed, Elizabeth, if you have very few students. The value system of the people here varies greatly from ours. They do not see the need, or the advantage, of spending many hours trying to learn about things they will never see nor know. What good is all that learning if it will not put food in the pot, or coax the fox to the trap?* [73–79]

Because . . . thou hast not asked riches, wealth, or honour, . . .
but hast asked wisdom and knowledge for thyself,
that thou mayest judge my people, . . .
wisdom and knowledge is granted unto thee;
and I will give thee riches, and wealth, and honour.
2 CHRONICLES 1:11–12

DISCOURAGEMENT

At the end of our first week of school we were down to thirteen students. At first I pretended they had some reason which kept them from the morning class. Nimmie knew better. She did not even seem surprised. Instead, she said with excitement, "Thirteen, Elizabeth! Thirteen. Can you believe it? We still have *thirteen* who are interested."

I wanted to argue with her. Thirteen was only about half of what we had started with.

By the end of the second week our number had dropped to five. Just five—when there was a village full of people who needed to learn to read and write. Nimmie was still not alarmed. "Five for our first year is wonderful. In the years to come the others will see the importance of knowing how to read, too."

I hoped Nimmie was right, but I was terribly disappointed. Wynn tried to encourage me, but he was also honest.

"I would like to believe that some might rejoin you, Elizabeth, but to be honest, I don't suppose they will. They have had no reason to believe that education from books will benefit them. That still has to be proven to them."

"But how can we show them?" I wailed.

"We can't—not overnight. It's going to take time." [87–91]

And let us not be weary in well doing:
for in due season we shall reap, if we faint not.
GALATIANS 6:9

PERSEVERANCE

Two days before Christmas, Wynn came home to find the students and me poring over our books.

"Aren't you even going to take a Christmas break?" Wynn asked after the students left.

The truth was, I couldn't bear to spend the days alone. My thoughts kept going home. I remembered the Christmases spent with my family in Toronto. When I visualized the preparations, my eyes would fill with tears. Then I would resolve to keep my thoughts on safer ground. I honestly would try, but soon I'd be seeing the red-bowed wrappings on the gifts stacked beneath the tree. I could see myself sitting at the table in our elegant dining room, head bowed while Father said the grace. Then as he carved the turkey we would chat and laugh, just for the joy of being alive and together.

I wept. I prayed. I felt I would never make it through this Christmas. Never in all of my life had I been so homesick.

Just hang on, I kept telling myself. *Soon it will be over and then you'll be all right again.* [96–97]

Forgetting those things which are behind,
and reaching forth unto those things which are before,
I press toward the mark for the prize
of the high calling of God.
PHILIPPIANS 3:13–14

IMMORTALITY

Wynn and I spent Christmas day before our fire. We had planned to go for a walk along the river, but the day turned out to be too cold for that. The day seemed long. There wasn't much to do except talk. We had few games to play, and no music.

While I prepared an evening snack of cold meat sandwiches and leftover pie, Wynn stretched out on the rug before the fire. By the time I returned to join him, he had fallen asleep. I knew my sleeping husband was tired. His job took so much of his time and energy. And after delivering a baby last night, he had been called to see a sick child.

He had lost weight, I noticed for the first time. I looked down at my own body. I too had lost a few pounds, which was reasonable. We were active and ate few foods that would add weight.

I looked at my hands. They were no longer the soft hands of a pampered woman. Time had changed us—time and the northland. [101–102]

Our bodies deteriorate in this life,
but in the life to come they will be transformed.
We shall all be changed. . . .
For this corruptible must put on incorruption,
and this mortal must put on immortality.
1 CORINTHIANS 15:52–53

A CALLING

Wynn took me gently in his arms and kissed away the tear that lay on my cheek.

"It's been tough this Christmas, hasn't it? I'm sorry you've been so lonesome."

"You noticed?"

"I noticed."

"I thought I was hiding it pretty well."

He hugged me closer. "I appreciate your trying, Beth, though I would have been more than happy to share it, to talk about it. It might have helped a bit. Sometimes I get lonesome, too."

I tightened my arms around him. Wynn, too, had family that he loved deeply. It wasn't easy for him to serve in the North. But the people here needed him. It was his commitment to them that kept him with the Force, that kept him here in the small settlement. Being a member of the Royal North West Mounted Police was more than a job. It was a calling to serve people. Wynn's even higher calling to serve his Lord was fulfilled in his responsibilities here among the trappers and Indians.

I reached up to kiss my husband, and with the kiss was a promise—a promise of my love and support for as long as he felt that the North needed him.   [105–106]

> *Whom he called, them he also justified:*
> *and whom he justified, them he also glorified. . . .*
> *If God be for us, who can be against us?*
> ROMANS 8:30–31

A FAMILY

We were a real family now. Wynn, me, and Susie. She had come to live with us after her mother had given birth to twins. Relatives had moved in to help care for the family, leaving no room for Susie. Wynn and I had been happy together, but a child was what we needed to make our life complete.

I looked at Wynn and the little girl on his knee. Their eyes were riveted to the pages of the storybook. My heart sang a little song. I loved Susie so much and I knew with certainty that she loved me in return. It was such fun to romp through the snow, to make cookies, to teach her to embroider. I thought ahead to all the things I still wanted to share with her.

And then a flash of insight shocked me back to reality.

I faced the fact that Susie would not be with us long. My heart ached as I formed the words: *She is not truly ours. She belongs to another family.* I knew this would not change, nor would I change it if I could. Susie loved her family, and they loved her. Ultimately she belonged with them.

I knew I must daily remind myself of this and do nothing that would make it any harder for Susie when she returned to her own home. My deep love must protect her from my love. It was an enigma, but I knew it was true. [114–115]

Children are an heritage of the Lord.
PSALM 127:3

BUILDING TOGETHER

Wynn and I talked after Susie went to bed about how God had been speaking to me. Wynn agreed that we needed to prepare Susie to return to her own world.

Our days changed, though our routine stayed much the same. I always went with her to gather the wood and take it to her house. While we chatted I tried to learn more about her people. When we went to her house I spent more time talking with her mother and the little boys.

At the end of the day when Wynn returned, Susie and Kip met him at the door. When Wynn took off his heavy boots, Susie ran to get his slippers. I made sure to leave plenty of time before supper for Wynn to read a story to Susie.

We said our table grace in her Indian language. We wanted Susie to feel it was not "the white man's God" we prayed to. He could be her God as well. And when we knelt for her bedtime prayer, we again prayed in words familiar to her.

We were building together now. We held her and loved her, cuddled and guided her, but all the time we did so it was with a consciousness that we were preparing her, and ourselves, for that inevitable day when our paths would separate and we would again walk down different trails. [116–117]

Train up a child in the way he should go:
and when he is old, he will not depart from it.
PROVERBS 22:6

133

CHRISTLIKENESS

Susie turned to Wynn. "It's not true, then? You don't lock children away so they never see their folks again?"

"You are right, Susie. We never lock children away."

"Then what do you do if they be bad?"

"We talk to the mothers and fathers and try to get them to help their children be good. We talk to the children and tell them all the dangers of continuing to be bad. We don't want children to grow up to be bad people. We don't like to lock up people—not anyone. But sometimes we have to keep grown-ups who insist on being bad from hurting other people."

Susie nodded her little dark head, very serious now. "You're like Jesus," she said thoughtfully.

Wynn's eyes widened. "Pardon me?"

"You're like Jesus," Susie said, more positively now that she had said the words out loud. "He doesn't like it when people be bad either. An' He doesn't like to send them away—out of heaven. But it would spoil heaven for everybody else if He let bad people in there."

Wynn said nothing, but his eyes looked misty as he reached out to tousle Susie's black hair. [124]

That Christ may dwell in your hearts by faith;
that ye, being rooted and grounded in love,
may . . . be filled with all the fulness of God.
EPHESIANS 3:17–19

DANGER

Men were running now, some toward the village and others toward the ice jam. What started as a leisurely excursion to watch the ice leave the river had turned into a nightmare. The ice had jammed, threatening to flood our village and destroy everything in it, including the people who had stayed behind.

I began to shake uncontrollably. Then I felt Susie patting my shoulder. "We need to pray," she whispered. "We need to pray quick. I don't want another father killed by the ice."

I pulled Susie to me and did as she suggested. Then Susie began to pray in her language. She implored the God who sent His Son Jesus to set free the river's waters. She reminded God that Wynn was like Jesus. And then she told God that she loved Him and would try her hardest, all her life, not to be bad. She said "Amen" in English to close her prayer.

The men had reached the water's edge. They lifted their rifles to their shoulders. Susie whispered, "Now, Jesus," and the air exploded. Ice flew in every direction, hundreds of feet into the air. For a few moments all was silent, and then a mighty cheer went up. The river was flowing again.

"He did it, Susie. He did it. Let's go meet Wynn."

Susie held back. "You said we're s'posed to say thank you."

Susie was right, and so we did. [127–129]

Call unto me, and I will answer thee,
and shew thee great and mighty things.
JEREMIAH 33:3

SORROW

Susie flitted through the summer like a pretty little butterfly. She had outgrown her few dresses, so I sewed her some more. I made them just like those of the other children—no frills, no ribbons. I wanted to make them feminine, but for Susie's sake I did not. It wasn't that I feared Susie would not like the new attire. I was afraid she might like the frills *too* much and find it difficult to return to simpler clothing.

Susie's return to her family came much sooner than we expected. In fact, Wynn wasn't even home the afternoon Susie had to leave to move with her family to the big village across the river. I had known she would eventually move home, but I had not prepared myself for the possibility that she might move away.

I chose the three books Susie loved and shoved them into her pack. "I want you to keep on reading," I said, "and to think of us. To remember all the good times we had here."

"I remember," she nodded, then closed the door quietly. It opened again, just a crack, and Susie said, "I forgot thanks." Then the door closed again.

I let the hot tears stream down my face. Susie was gone. Just like that. Gone with her own people, back to her own world.

[133-138]

> *Neither death nor life . . .*
> *nor things present, nor things to come . . .*
> *shall be able to separate us from the love of God.*
> ROMANS 8:38–39

GOOD GIFTS

Wynn and I fell into a routine, and I was thankful for all the activities that filled my days. Still I thought about Susie and her mother. Had I done enough? Said enough? Did Susie know how a Christian was to live out her faith? Did her mother really understand about God's plan of salvation? Had I made it plain that it was for her, too? Nagging thoughts picked away at me. I prayed and prayed for the family.

Then one day as I was praying, God spoke to my heart.

Do you think I am unaware of where they are? He seemed to gently say. *Do you think I have deserted them? Don't you think that I care, that my love is certainly as strong as yours? And don't you know that I, through my Holy Spirit, can go on talking to them, even in your absence?*

I felt humbled. Of course I knew all that. Susie's nurture did not depend on me. Nor did her mother's salvation. It had depended on God all along. Where they lived had nothing to do with it. Now I committed them totally to God and let the guilt and fear slip from my shoulders. [140–141]

If ye then, being evil,
know how to give good gifts unto your children:
how much more shall your heavenly Father
give the Holy Spirit to them that ask him?
LUKE 11:13

GOD'S CARE

The man reached into his leather jacket and withdrew a folded sheet of paper. He said not a word, just handed it to me, turned on his heel, and left.

I closed the door and went to the table, looking at the unfamiliar note I held. I finally found my sense and spread it out on the table. It was a simple letter written on paper torn from a child's work scribbler. I flipped it over; it was signed "Susie."

My heart beat faster as I read. Susie's printing had improved; she had not forgotten what she had been taught.

"How are you. I am good. My mother is good two. We have a church here. I go. My mother gos two. We like it. We have a school here. Many boys and girls go. The teacher is nice, but not as nice as you. My mother feels better she says to say thank you. She didn't know before to say that. I miss you and Kip and Mr. Wynn. Did my garden grow okay. Susie."

I read the letter three times before I let the tears fall. She was fine! Our Susie was fine! She was in school, and in church, too. A voice within me seemed to say, "*See, I am caring for her,*" and I bowed my head in thankfulness to acknowledge that care.

Though the winter storm had intensified, rattling the windows in fury, it could not bother me. I felt warm and content. God was taking good care of our Susie. [141–142]

Casting all your care upon him;
for he careth for you.
1 PETER 5:7

YEARNING

Pregnant with her third child, Nimmie was feeling sick. I offered to take Nonita home with me to care for her, but Nimmie insisted the little girl was no trouble.

"Then I'll come over and give you a hand here," I told her.

And so through the wintry months of January and February, I trudged off to Nimmie's almost every day to help with laundry, dishes, and baby care.

On many days Nimmie was forced to stay in bed. She usually took baby Sonny with her. He seemed to rest better cuddled up against her. While they slept I did Nimmie's work and played with Nonita. What a little dear she was. I found myself eager to get to Nimmie's each day just so I could spend time with the child.

At our supper table I shared with Wynn all of the funny things she said and did that day. We laughed about them together.

Being with Nimmie's babies did not lessen my ache for a child of my own but, rather, increased it. Each day I would petition God's throne for the child I still did not have. My heart grew heavier and heavier. It seemed I had been praying for a baby forever, and God still had not heard my prayer. [144–145]

If we ask any thing according to his will, he heareth us:
And if we know that he hears us . . . we know that we have
the petitions that we desired of him.
1 JOHN 5:15

FORESIGHT

The first of March ushered in a terrible storm that lasted for four days. In spite of the weather, Wynn decided he should go see how people in the village were faring.

The news was not good. Many people lay huddled together under all the furs and blankets they owned. Two elderly women had already died from exposure. In some cabins they had not been able to keep the fires going, and without fires there was no food, so those who were not well were getting even weaker.

Wynn was going to haul wood to the homes where it was needed and asked me if I would make some stew or soup that he could take to the hungry.

I hastened to comply. It wasn't long until I heard Wynn and the complaining dogs outside our cabin. I knew Wynn was taking from our winter's wood supply to build fires in some of the other homes. If only the Indian people could be convinced to bring in a wood supply each fall and stack it by their doors, but to them that was unnecessary work. After all, they reasoned, the wood was always right there in the nearby thicket. [145–146]

Go to the ant . . . consider her ways, and be wise:
which having no guide, overseer, or ruler,
provideth her meat in the summer,
and gathereth her food in the harvest.
PROVERBS 6:6–8

LOSS

When the storm finally ended I breathed a sigh of relief, but it was premature. Sickness hit the village. Wynn worked almost around the clock. I made soup and stew, kettle by kettle, and we carried it to those who could not manage by themselves.

The few who remained healthy helped us care for the sick. Ian carried wood and water and brought food supplies from his store. But then Nimmie and the family became sick, and he was needed at home.

I called on Nimmie often. She was so sick I feared we would lose her. She did miscarry the baby, but she fought tenaciously for her own life. I worried about the weak and sickly Sonny. Surely his frail body could not withstand this additional illness.

But, strangely, it was darling little Nonita whom we lost. I would have cried for days had I not been needed so desperately. As it was I could only ache. Nimmie's little herb-gatherer, her little sunshine, was gone.

With heavy hearts we tried to strengthen one another. Little Nonita's laughter and chatter was only a memory. I think Nimmie was glad even for Sonny's fussing. It gave her a good excuse to constantly hold him. Nimmie greatly needed her arms full during those difficult days. [147–148]

And God shall wipe away all tears from their eyes;
and there shall be no more death, neither sorrow, nor crying.
REVELATION 21:4

EMPTINESS

Guess what," Nimmie said excitedly, but didn't give me any time for a guess. "We're going to have another baby!"

I was happy for Nimmie, really I was, but at the same time my own heart felt a pang of disappointment. Here it was again! I was called on to share the happiness of another who was given the very thing I longed for so desperately.

I managed a smile, gave Nimmie a hug, and offered to fix us some tea.

"I can't stay," Nimmie said. "I left Sonny with Ian. The little rascal will be pulling things off the shelves. But I just couldn't wait to tell you. I know you grieved for Nonita almost as much as I did. It was so hard to lose her, Elizabeth. I thought I wouldn't be able to bear it. And now God is sending me another child! I can hardly wait. This baby won't take Nonita's place, but it will fill a big emptiness in my heart."

It was the first Nimmie had talked to me about losing Nonita. I knew that her heart ached, that she grieved. But she tried so hard to be brave. And now, as she said, the emptiness was about to be filled.

My own emptiness remained. I turned so that Nimmie would not spot my brimming eyes and trembling lips. [150]

Rejoice with them that do rejoice.
ROMANS 12:15

WELCOME

Sonny pulled the dish of cookies onto the floor before either Nimmie or I could make a grab for it. Nimmie sat him in the corner and was cleaning up the mess when a strange look came over her face.

"What is it?" I asked, worried that she had hurt herself.

She straightened slowly. "I think it is time, Elizabeth."

I didn't stop to ask her more. I ran through the side door into the store. Ian went to get the midwife, and I ran back to assist Nimmie into bed.

"I'll take Sonny home with me," I assured her when Ian and the midwife arrived.

I bundled up the small Sonny and bid Nimmie goodbye. I hoped it would not be long until we heard good news. I thought Nimmie was probably hoping for another little herb-gatherer, though she had not said.

We had finished our supper when Ian came for Sonny, his face broad with a grin.

"Another boy," he beamed. "Alexander." I wondered if Nimmie shared his great joy. Then I decided that she certainly would. She would welcome whom God chose to send. [160]

As one whom his mother comforteth,
so will I comfort you.
ISAIAH 66:13

143

WORRY

I visited Nimmie and her new baby frequently. He was a lovely, healthy boy and seemed to have grown each time I went to see him. Alexander was a contented baby with a chubby little face and dimples. His dark eyes watched your face and his small fists knotted themselves at the front of your gown. I loved him, almost as if he were my own.

I held him and thought of the sweet little Nonita and my heart ached. Was it possible that in the days ahead fever again might strike the village and this one, too, would be taken? *Does Nimmie ever think these thoughts?* I wondered. *Maybe I should be glad that I've never had a child. I don't think I could stand to have one and then lose it.* I couldn't imagine anything harder to bear.

But Nimmie made no reference to fear. Daily she thanked God for her new baby.

[161]

In every thing give thanks:
for this is the will of God in Christ Jesus concerning you.
1 THESSALONIANS 5:18

WITCHCRAFT

Little Deer was over for tea one day and mentioned a woman who has special herbs to help one to—to—" I faltered. I wasn't sure how to continue. "For those who do not have children," I finally said. "She said she has helped women in the village."

"Is it Big Woman?" Wynn asked.

"Yes," I answered, somewhat startled that he was so far ahead of me. "You knew about it?"

"No, but I'm not surprised. Big Woman will promise anything for a little money."

I was a bit put out with Wynn. Didn't he think a baby was worth a little money?

"City doctors want money, too," I reminded him.

"But they're not witch doctors," Wynn stated simply.

I sank back against my pillow. In my desperation I had nearly consulted a witch doctor. I had rationalized that a little chant could do no harm. Yet I knew that witchcraft was wrong. No wonder I had felt uneasy! Then I realized that not once had I prayed about it. If I had prayed I would have known. Yet even in my ignorance and waywardness, God had protected me.[163]

There shall not be found among you any one that. . .
useth divination, or an observer of times,
or an enchanter, or a witch, . . . For all that do these things
are an abomination unto the Lord.
DEUTERONOMY 18:10, 12

NERVOUSNESS

Wynn decided I should see a doctor in Calgary to determine if there was a physical problem keeping me from becoming pregnant. The report was good, in a way. The doctor could find no reason that I could not conceive. But since there was no problem, that also meant there was nothing he could do for me. I might as well not have come—except that it had been wonderful seeing my family.

I settled back into the routine of village living with a light heart, but I continued to argue with God. Didn't Hannah receive the child she had prayed for? Weren't there numerous women in the world who had children they did not really want nor care for? Did the whole thing seem reasonable? Why shouldn't those who would love and protect the child be the ones to give birth? And why not me? Why should I be denied?

I tried to push the thoughts from me, but daily they nagged at me, eventually making me nervous and listless. I lost weight. I did not sleep well. I found no answers. [194]

The Lord had shut up [Hannah's] womb. . . .
Therefore she wept, and did not eat. . . .
And she . . . prayed unto the Lord, and wept sore. . . .
Then Eli answered and said, Go in peace:
the God of Israel grant Thee thy petition.
1 SAMUEL 1:6–17

SAMUEL

One dark evening as Wynn and I sat before our fire expecting the winter's first snowfall, we heard a shuffling at our door. It was a young man whose wife had been ill. He nodded solemnly to Wynn and then crossed the room to where I sat.

"You keep," he said, holding his baby out to me. "She gone now. I go trap." He placed the baby in my arms and then left.

I stared after him, not knowing what I was to do.

"What did he mean?" I asked, my voice full of wonder.

"He lost his wife," said Wynn. "He has to go to his trapline. He wants you to keep the baby."

Tears began to trickle down my face. I cried for the young father. His eyes had been filled with pain when he handed me his child. I cried for the mother who had fought so hard but had died so young. I cried for the baby who had been left motherless at such an early age. And I cried for me, tears of joy, because I now held a baby in my arms, a baby to love and care for. I held him close and thanked God for answering my prayers.

We named the baby Samuel. It seemed fitting. Hannah had named her baby Samuel after God had answered her prayer. The name meant "asked of God," and every time I said the name I was reminded again of the miracle of Samuel coming to us. [198–199]

Hannah . . . bare a son, and called his name Samuel,
saying, Because I have asked him of the Lord.
1 SAMUEL 1:20

Wynn and I loved and cared for little Samuel as though he was our own, thanking God every day for the opportunity. When spring came and the other trappers returned home, I expected Samuel's father to come and visit him. But he didn't.

We celebrated Samuel's first birthday by taking him to the wilderness for a picnic. Samuel seemed to love every part of the great outdoors.

Two days after our celebration, Samuel's father finally came. But not to visit his son. He came to take him away to his new village.

I started to cry—deep, agonizing sobs that shook my whole body. Wynn moved to comfort me, to hold me in his arms, and then I realized that Wynn was weeping, too. I don't suppose anything would have brought me to my senses more quickly. Knowing of Wynn's deep pain brought me out of myself. Wynn needed me. We needed each other. We were losing our baby.

For a moment I hated the young man. How could he do such a thing? And then, I dared to go a step further. I became very angry at God. Why was He letting such a thing happen? I tried to push the anger from me, knowing that it wasn't right, but it would not go away. [208–213]

Rest in the Lord, and wait patiently for him. . .
Cease from anger, and forsake wrath.
PSALM 37:7–8

VOID

The next weeks were the worst days of my life. I wandered in an empty world, void of feeling except for pain. The house was empty, Samuel's bed was empty, my life was empty.

At times I tried to pray, but God seemed far away. I didn't even feel close to Wynn. He quietly went about his daily tasks. I tended to mine. He tried to communicate, to hold me, to get me to talk it out, but I resisted, putting him off with one flimsy excuse or another.

I lost weight, which was not surprising. I wasn't eating. I still couldn't sleep. I just lay in bed at night, wondering what was happening to Samuel.

When winter's snow swept in, burying all the uncleanness of the village beneath a blanket of white, I watched without comment. *It would be nice,* I thought, *to be able to bury one's feelings as completely.*

But God had not forgotten me. Day by day snatches of scripture verses chipped away at the hardness of my heart. Little phrases and promises began to come to my mind. There were those who prayed, I know, and perhaps it was in response to them that the Lord kept working with me. I knew it was also because I was His child and He loved me. [217–218]

*For we have not an high priest which cannot be touched
with the feeling of our infirmities.*
HEBREWS 4:15

As I looked at the snow lying cold and clean on the village paths, I thought of the verse, "Wash me, and I shall be whiter than snow." I didn't feel clean now. I felt defiled. Dirty. Angry and bitter.

"As your child, I thought you would shield me, God. But here I am—all alone and hurting."

For the Lord your God is a merciful God; he will not forsake you or destroy you.

"But I feel forsaken, Lord, and empty."

Call on me, and I will answer you, and show you great and mighty things, which you do not know.

"Could you, Lord? Could you lift this burden from my heart and make life meaningful again?"

For you shall go out with joy, and be led out with peace; the mountains and the hills shall break forth into singing before you, and all the trees of the field shall clap their hands.

That was what I needed, what I longed for. Perhaps it wasn't the absence of Samuel that was making my life so miserable, but the absence of the presence of God. I took my Bible and went to my bedroom. I would spend as long on my knees as necessary to find and restore the peace with Him that I had known. [218–219]

> *Cast me not away from thy presence;*
> *and take not thy holy spirit from me.*
> PSALM 51:11

REPENTANCE

I cried out in repentance, and all of the bitterness began to melt. I told God that I accepted His plan for my life, even if it meant I would be childless, and that I would stop fighting it and leave things in His hands. I no longer wanted to be miserable or to bring misery to others. I thought of Wynn and the pain I had caused him. I asked the Lord to forgive me, and I vowed to ask Wynn to forgive me also.

I prayed for Samuel and for his father—that he would be good and wise, and that he might be given the opportunity to know the Lord so that he could introduce Samuel to the Savior.

I talked to God about many things, keeping nothing back, and by the time I rose from my knees I felt clean and at peace again.

I knew there still would be days ahead when I might wish for a child. I would take those days as they came, asking God to help me through them, but I would not chafe nor be impatient and insistent. With God's help I would look for the joy in life that He would choose to give me. It was foolish to go through life pouting and complaining and making myself miserable when I already had so much to be thankful for. I would make each day an experience with the Lord. I would find many things to thank Him for. I started out by thanking Him for Wynn. [220]

For godly sorrow worketh repentance.
2 CORINTHIANS 7:10

NECESSITIES

When Wynn's new posting came, he decided not to take it. "I'll ask for a post back in civilization," he explained. "The North has been hard on you, Elizabeth. You've been asked to give so much, and you've always been willing, but it's time now—"

I did not let Wynn finish. "You know, it was good for me to make that trip to Calgary. I found out that stores and sidewalks and even bathrooms aren't necessary for life after all."

"You're saying you don't want to go back?" Wynn asked.

"I'm not saying I couldn't enjoy living there, but that I don't need it to be happy. I can be happy here just as well. The important thing is being with you."

"But I'd be with you."

"In body maybe, but your heart would still be in the North. Neither of us would be happy under those circumstances. Let's take that posting—while we are young and healthy and want to do it. The people need us, Wynn."

"You're sure?"

"Perfectly sure."

And I was. With Wynn's arms around me and God's peace in my heart, I had no reason to fear anything the future might hold.   [222-223]

For he satisfieth the longing soul,
and filleth the hungry soul with goodness.
PSALM 107:9

WHEN HOPE

SPRINGS NEW

ANTICIPATION

Is it much farther?" I felt like a child asking again, but I couldn't help myself. Agitation filled my whole being each time we topped a hill, and the settlement was still not in view.

Wynn smiled. "Not too far," he comforted.

"How many hills?" I asked, hoping to pin him down.

Now he chuckled. "You sound like a kid," he teased.

I did sound like a kid. It seemed as if we had been on the trail forever. It had only been four days, but it felt like weeks.

Wynn squeezed my hand. "I'll go see what I can find out from the guide."

He wasn't gone long. "You'll be happy to know that we should be there in about forty-five minutes!" He gave my shoulders a hug and then was gone again.

Forty-five minutes. Even that sounded like a long time. I forced myself to think of our new home at Smoke Lake. I was looking forward to a nice hot bath and a chance to sleep in a real bed. Mosquito netting on the windows and door for privacy would seem like luxuries after this trip—with its heat, rain, and wind; with its steep hills, flat marshlands, dusty trails, and soggy gumbo. But it would not be long now.   [11–13]

> *According to his promise,*
> *[we] look for new heavens and a new earth,*
> *wherein dwelleth righteousness.*
> 2 PETER 3:13

ANXIETY

During our four days of travel I had acquired aching bones, a sunburned nose, and a multitude of mosquito and blackfly bites. But it wasn't these irritations that troubled me the most. My agitation—that hollow, knotted spot in the center of my stomach—was all due to my fear of the unknown.

The wagons up ahead paused on the brow of the hill. I knew without even asking that just down that hill lay our new settlement—our new home. I wanted to see it, yet I held back in fear. How could one be so torn up inside, wanting to run to see what lay before, yet holding back from looking, all at the same time?

Without comment, Wynn reached forward and took my hand, then bowed his head and addressed our Father simply. "Our Father in heaven, we come to this new assignment not knowing what is ahead. Only You know the needs of these people. Help us to meet those needs. Help us to be caring, compassionate and kind. Help Elizabeth with all the new adjustments. Give her fellowship and friendships. Give her a ministry to the people, and keep us close to one another and to You. Amen."

I felt better after Wynn's prayer, but it was also another reminder of all the new experiences lying ahead.   [12–15]

> *For I know the thoughts that I think toward you,*
> *saith the Lord, thoughts of peace, and not of evil.*
> JEREMIAH 29:11

DISMAY

Surely there must be some mistake. That cabin isn't large enough for Wynn's office, let alone our household. I had expected something better than such crowded, miserable quarters. I recovered as quickly as I could, gulped away the tears, and tried to speak. "We'll manage," was all I could say.

With new determination I lifted my chin, took Kip on his leash, and started down a winding trail that led out of the village. When we finally reached the woods beyond the village, I slowed my pace and took a deep breath of the fresh summer air. It was tangy with the smell of pine trees and flowers. A small stream trickled nearby, and I followed the path that led along the bank.

We had not gone far when we came to a small lake. I looked across it, enjoying its beauty, its tranquility. Here was a hallowed spot in the middle of all the squalor and disappointment of the village. Here was a place where I could refresh my soul. I eased myself down on the grass beside the water and let my frustration and loneliness drain from me.

Surely God is in this place. The words formed in my mind without conscious effort. As I repeated them, peacefulness settled upon me. "Surely, God is in this place." I spoke the words aloud. It was true. It was a promise. It was enough. [18–21]

Lord, thou hast been our dwelling place
in all generations.
PSALM 90:1

RESPONSIBILITY

You're the first white woman to live in this village, Elizabeth," Wynn told me.

"I am?" Suddenly I felt a heavy responsibility. The people would judge the whole white race by what they saw in me.

Would I be worthy? Would I be able to contribute to their way of life? Or would I appear to threaten it? Would I fit in where no white woman had been before? Would the Indian women feel free to come and sip tea? Or would they see me as a strange creature with odd ways who should be shunned and avoided?

I did not have answers to any of those questions. I looked at the small space around me. I knew without visiting the other homes that this one was much like theirs. I smiled, beginning to feel some comfort in my strange, new home. If I lived like they lived, surely it would not be as difficult for me to cross the barriers. If my floor was dirt, if my stove was small, if my bed stood in the corner of the same room, then wouldn't the Indian women find it easier to accept me?

Wynn must have noticed my smile. He lifted his head and looked at me, the question showing in his eyes.

"Well, I might be white, but my home will be no different. Perhaps that will make it easier to become one of them." [26]

I am made all things to all men,
that I might by all means save some.
1 CORINTHIANS 9:22

COMPANIONSHIP

I met two women from the village as I walked to the trading post. I smiled and greeted them in their own language, but they avoided eye contact and passed on, looking almost frightened. I entered the store by its one low door and looked around. The trader eyed me shrewdly.

"I need eggs," I said, using the unfamiliar Indian words.

"No eggs," he informed me.

"I also need some lard."

"No lard," he stated.

"Oh, my," I said in English. "What am I going to do now?"

"What you say?" he asked in the Indian dialect.

I tried to explain that I had been speaking to myself.

"When in here, best you speak to me—not you."

I had the feeling I wasn't going to care too much for this surly man with his unkempt appearance and piercing eyes. I nodded and headed for the door. I didn't want to go back to my small, confined cabin, but I realized that I wasn't going to find what I was looking for here. What I wanted more than eggs or lard was companionship.   [31–33]

And Abraham believed God. . .
and he was called the Friend of God.
JAMES 2:23

SELF-PITY

As I ducked out the door of the trading post, I heard two Indian women chatting. "Why pale-faced one with dog child go there?" I knew immediately they were talking about me. They had seen me fluff, brush, and bathe Kip. And they had seen us take him into our small cabin while their dogs spent the days and nights, rain or shine, out-of-doors. Apparently they had concluded that I had substituted a dog for the child I did not have.

How could they actually think that Kip, as much as I loved him, could take the place of the child I longed for? If only they knew my pain. I walked briskly, tears streaming down my cheeks, praying as I walked. I had never thought it possible to be so lonely, so shut off from one's world.

At length I was able to get a firm hold on my emotions. I decided I would not engage in self-pity even though the days ahead did look bleak. *I have my Lord,* I told myself. *He has promised to be with me even to the end of the world.* For a few moments I felt that I must indeed be very near to the end of the world, my world, but I jacked up my courage. God had promised He would never leave me nor forsake me. That held true on a city street, in a rural teacherage, or in a remote part of the North. [46-48]

> *And David was greatly distressed;*
> *for the people spake of stoning him, . . .*
> *but David encouraged himself in the Lord.*
> 1 SAMUEL 30:6

TRADITIONS

Our Indian neighbors enjoyed much more social life than had the people in Beaver River. We often heard the beating of the drums as they conducted one ceremony or another.

At first the strange drumbeats and the rising and falling chants wafting over the night stillness seemed eery. The sounds reminded me that we were the outsiders here. We were in the midst of a different culture from our own. To us, the chants and drumbeats were distracting noise, but to the Indians these symbolized their religion, their very being. They believed in the magic and supernatural power of the chants and dances.

As far as we knew, the Indians in this remote yet rather large village had never seen a Christian missionary nor been introduced to his God. The old ways were never questioned and were held to with strict rigidity. The rain fell or the killing frost descended in accordance with the pleasure of the spirits, so it behooved the people to do all in their power to keep those gods happy with age-old ritual and age-old worship.   [51]

Beware lest any man spoil you through philosophy
and vain deceit, after the tradition of men, . . .
and not after Christ.
COLOSSIANS 2:8

161

PERSECUTION

I should not have been surprised when word filtered back to me of the Indian women's fear that association with the "pale-faced" woman might bring down the wrath of the gods. There didn't seem to be any consensus as to why the spirits might object, but the elders informed the younger, and the younger warned their children, and the villagers, with one accord, were afraid to test the conviction. I could think of nothing I could do to break the barrier except wait. Surely in time they would see that I did not invoke the anger of their gods.

The Indian people of this tribe had a strange conception concerning the rule of the Mountie. To them he represented the law, and law was closely tied to payment for sins committed. The gods frowned upon wrongdoing and reacted with a vengeance when one stepped out of line. Therefore, in some strange, invisible way, the white lawman might have connections with the super powers. They treated Wynn with both deference and fear. As Wynn's wife, I was suspect.

Understanding the reasons for the shunning helped my peace of mind. At least I did not feel rejected on a personal level. I prayed about it and left the entire matter in God's hands, asking Him, in the meantime, for patience and understanding.   [53]

> Blessed are ye, when men shall revile you,
> and persecute you, and shall say all manner
> of evil against you falsely, for my sake.
> MATTHEW 5:11

CONDESCENSION

D o you think they'll ever accept us?" I asked Wynn. "As part of them, I mean, not as the 'Force'?"

"I don't know, Elizabeth. They don't know much about the white man here. They don't have anything to base their trust on yet."

"But wasn't there a Mountie here before us?"

"Yes, but that might be some of the problem."

"You mean they had a 'bad' officer?"

"No, not bad. He did his duty honestly enough. But he held himself apart from the people. He might have even taken advantage of their belief that he might be—uh—different. If they wanted to think he was in cahoots with the spirits, that was fine with him. I don't mean that he fostered it. But he didn't mind if the Indian people thought him a little different—a little above them."

"But why?"

"Some men just like having authority. He didn't like to be bothered. One way to keep the villagers at a distance was to keep them believing that there was a 'great gulf' between them and him." [58–59]

For I say . . . to every man that is among you,
not to think of himself more highly than he ought.
ROMANS 12:3

BARRIER

We learned too late that the small island Wynn and I chose for my garden had been the site where an unpopular medicine man had lived and died. The Indians avoided it because they were afraid of it, but not because they thought it was sacred.

I thought about that. Certainly I was not afraid of this bit of ground. It was part of God's creation. If He chose to grant me a good garden here, I would accept it as from His hand.

While Wynn and I prepared the soil, we felt eyes watching us from the trees. "See," I wanted to shout, "there is no curse on this ground. The power of the medicine man does not compare to the power of the One True God who created this soil and planted these grasses." But I said nothing. I prayed that time might prove it to the people.

But I did feel sorry that we had inadvertently placed another barrier between ourselves and the people. We wanted to help them, live with them, and be their friends, but we could not because of all their religious taboos.

"I guess we won't need to build a fence to keep anyone out," Wynn teased.

"Oh, Wynn, I hope this doesn't cause you any trouble."

"We didn't do it intentionally, Elizabeth. And who knows, God might use it for good." [67]

For every creature of God is good, and nothing to be refused,
if it be received with thanksgiving.
1 TIMOTHY 4:4

INTERCESSION

One day as I walked to my garden I heard the words "bad omen" and knew they were spoken in reference to me. I wanted to eavesdrop further, but I forced myself to keep walking. All the time I was in the garden, I prayed. Though I hardly knew what to say.

"Lord," I said, "I really don't understand what is going on here. The people of the village are so steeped in their pagan belief that they think the drought has come as a punishment to me for planting my garden here—and all of them will have to suffer for it. I don't know how to help them, but I don't want to be guilty of driving them even further from You. The reasonable thing would seem to be for You to send rain. That would water the ground, replenish the food supply for the animals, and fill our stream again. It should help our problem with the villagers, too. Then they might understand that I really had nothing to do with the drought. But I leave it in Your hands, God. Help me to be patient and to do things Your way. I can't untangle this myself. Thank You, Lord, for hearing me. Amen."

A strange peace came to my soul. I had the assurance that God had heard my prayer and was going to act on my behalf, though I didn't know how. [78–79]

We know not what we should pray for as we ought:
but the Spirit itself maketh intercession for us.
ROMANS 8:26

Wynn came home as dry as he had left.

"What's with the water barrel?" he asked.

"When I was praying this morning, asking God to break the barrier between us and the people, I felt strongly that He was going to answer my prayer. I feel sure that He will send rain."

Wynn smiled and whispered, "Well, praise God." Then he looked back at the rickety barrel. "I'm not sure how much that poor old barrel will hold, though. If you'll get some rags, I'll get the tar, and we'll stuff those holes the best we can."

All night I expected to hear rain. Even in my sleep, I kept one ear attuned. No rain fell. I was sure I would waken to clouded skies, but the sun shone brightly in the morning.

"I don't understand, Lord," I whispered.

"Be patient," came back the inward reply.

"Lord, give me the patience!" I cried. "I have never been patient. You know that."

"Then trust Me," said the inner voice. *"You have always been able to trust."*

"Lord, I trust You." I knew as I said the words that they came from an honest heart. I did trust Him! I might not understand His workings, but I did trust His ways.   [80–81]

> For my thoughts are not your thoughts,
> neither are your ways my ways, saith the Lord.
> ISAIAH 55:8

EXPECTATION

All that day I watched for rain. Nothing happened. That night I again lay awake, but there was not a hint of a storm.

The next day was even hotter. As usual, I took Kip and went to the garden, talking to God all the way there.

"Lord, this pail in my hand does not mean that I don't trust You. I know that You are going to answer my prayer. Bringing rain seems like the logical way for You to do it, Lord—but it might not be. In the meantime, I think You expect me to do my part, so I will continue to water my garden—until You tell me not to."

Even with my careful ministrations, the plants were suffering from the drought. Carrying the water was back-breaking work, but I continued until I could do no more. I soaked and soaked the earth, pouring on bucketful after bucketful.

Finally I stood to rest and looked heavenward again. A strange cloud was forming in the east. Would our rain come from the east instead of the west or north as usual? I smiled. Wasn't that just like the Lord, to do something out of the ordinary so there would be no doubt that it had come from Him?   [83–84]

My soul, wait thou only upon God;
for my expectation is from him.
PSALM 62:5

HELP

I was almost to our cabin when I heard children calling, "Fire!"

I looked to the east again. The strange cloud. Of course, it was smoke. Panic seized me. Wynn was away, and most of the other men were attending a feast and a rain dance two days away. When I reached the village, the trader was outside.

"How much time?" I asked.

"Hard to say," Mr. LaMeche answered. "Could travel fast. If rain not come soon whole village be burned. We can only run—or fry like chickens."

"Run where?"

"I do not know."

I looked to the west, still expecting rain clouds. But the sky was clear. All around me frightened people milled about, but no one took charge. I could hear the crackling flames and the snap of large pine trees being split open by the intense heat. Burning debris, carried forward by driving wind, planted new fires, leading the way for the giant flames leaping behind them.

"Father," I prayed, my voice breaking, "I don't understand this, but I do trust You. What do I do now?"   [85–87]

> *To whom will ye flee for help?*
> ISAIAH 10:3
>
> *My help cometh from the Lord.*
> PSALM 121:2

ACTION

I ran toward the trading post. Without waiting for Mr. LaMeche to say anything, I flung an order his way. "Put harness on horses and hook to wagons. I find drivers." Then I ran on. To a group of frightened women, I called, "Gather everything you can. Then go to lake." They stared at me without moving. "Go!" I yelled. "Do what I say!"

I ran toward a group of young boys. "You and you, run to corrals and help trader. Then drive through village, gather all who cannot walk, and go to lake." They, too, just stared. "Go!" I said, pushing them in the right direction. I turned to the other boys. "Tell everyone in village to grab what they can and run to lake. Hurry!"

Soon the village was alive with activity. I got a team of horses to our cabin and, with God's help, also got them hitched to the wagon. A young woman offered to hold the horses while I got cooking pots.

"Don't wait," I called. "Drive to lake. Drive out far in lake." She nodded and was gone. I grabbed whatever my hands touched and threw it onto blankets. Then I wrapped it into one large backpack and started for the lake.

"Oh, God, may everyone be at the lake." Then my cry changed. "Help me make it, God. Help me make it." [87–90]

> *Make haste to help me,*
> *O Lord my salvation.*
> PSALM 38:22

A voice coached me as I ran. Hands reached to me from the darkness. Then I felt the merciful coolness of the water. "Thank You. I made it," I breathed, sinking to my knees. Behind us the flames roared and crackled.

"Did we get everyone?"

"I think so," LaMeche replied.

"Thank God!" I sighed. "Will stream stop fire before it gets to lake?"

"No. Wind blows too hard. Stream is too dry."

I began to pray again. But still there was no rain. The flames drove relentlessly toward us. But then, a strange thing happened. We all saw it; yet none could believe it. Suddenly, the wind changed direction, driving the flames toward the area that had already been consumed. Within moments the fire lost some of its ferocity.

The fire still crackled, but the heat was not as intense. Soon we could leave the cold water. I breathed a prayer of thankfulness.

[90–94]

The name of the Lord is a strong tower:
the righteous runneth into it, and is safe.
PROVERBS 18:10

ASSURANCE

As soon as LaMeche started toward the wagons, the people took it as a signal to leave the water. With one accord we waded toward shore. Shivering in my wet clothes, I pondered the irony of the situation. Moments ago, flames had destroyed my home, and already I was longing for a fire.

In the eery light from the still-burning fire, people began to search for belongings they had dropped by the lakeshore.

Using all the blankets we could find, we worked together to make beds for the children, the sick, and the elderly. The rest of us huddled around fires for warmth, still too stunned to talk. As the night wore on, we took turns adding sticks to the fire.

Here and there people curled upon the sand beside the fires and attempted to get some sleep. I told myself that I should walk through the camp to see how everyone was faring. If Wynn were present, he would do that. I didn't seem able to move. Totally exhausted, I shivered again and wished for morning.

Slowly, nature began returning to normal. The wind slackened; the stars came out; an owl hooted; a fish jumped. Then, from somewhere, LaMeche produced a pot of coffee. It seemed to be a promise that the rest of the world would one day be normal again as well. Somehow we all would make it through this nightmare.   [94–96]

The Lord is not slack concerning his promise.
2 PETER 3:9

NEEDS

When the dawn began to break, we could see smoke still curling as the fires smoldered. The blackened, desolate area that had been our village was not visible to us because of the trees that still stood between us and the settlement. Perhaps it was a mercy of God that it was hidden from us.

I hated to leave the warmth of the fire. My clothing was still wet, and I felt chilled even though I had been by the fire most of the night. Yet, when the camp began to stir, I knew that I, too, would need to get on my feet. It was a new day, and we had many challenges facing us. Here were almost two hundred people with no homes, no clothing except what we wore, and no food to fill our empty stomachs.

I walked back and forth before the small campfire. I worked my arms and legs and rubbed at my back—all the time thinking and praying. I could not have said where my thoughts ended and prayers began—they seemed to be one and the same.

"Lord, we need food. I don't know where we are going to get it. But You know. Show me how to care for these people. Give me wisdom—and, Lord, give me help. I can't do it on my own." [97–98]

Take no thought for your life, what ye shall eat. . . .
Behold the fowls of the air. . . .
Your heavenly Father feedeth them.
MATTHEW 6:25–26

GOD'S RESOURCES

A voice behind me made me jump.

"Yours? I think so."

"You found it!" I cried with joy.

"Lucky for you, you drop it this side of stream." A twinkle appeared in LaMeche's eyes. I had never seen him show even the hint of a smile before. "A surprise you could run at all," he joked. "You must bring everything but iron bed."

"You are right," I said, attempting to laugh. I set my bundle of blankets on the ground and spread it open.

"How are the people?" I asked.

"Good. No one not here."

What a relief. I tried to get my thoughts in order. "I must go to island—to check garden. I'll be back with some food."

My garden was limp and parched. And yet there seemed to be life in many of the plants. Then I remembered the thorough watering of the day before. I had soaked and soaked them, though I had not understood why at the time. But God knew. He had prompted me to water my vegetables. I looked at them with thanksgiving, but I wondered how so few vegetables could feed so many hungry people.

"Trust Me," again came the words.   [98–101]

So the men sat down . . . about five thousand.
And Jesus took the [two] loaves . . . and . . . the [five] fishes . . .
[and] they were filled.
JOHN 6:10–12

COMPLIMENT

Finally the rain came. Our fire sputtered and died. Now we would have to manage without even its small comfort. LaMeche stared ahead, saying nothing. I hated being so cut off from another human being. I tried for conversation.

"I am glad for all your help today," I said. "I don't know what I do without you."

There was no reply.

"When I get up in morning and look at all people, I don't know what to do, so I pray. I ask God what to do—but I ask for more. I ask Him for help. And He answer me. He send you."

"You are stubborn woman," LaMeche finally said, but there was no malice in his words. "You get people to lake, and give vegetables from garden. You saved village, you know?"

"Not true, I only—"

He broke in. "No one else think. We all run in circles. Now you sit in rain while everyone else sleeps. Women. They are strange creatures. They want most, but accept least. You make fancy curtains, brush dog, fix hair. But then, when there is nothing, you give away little you have. I had forgotten. It was way of my mother also. She Indian, but she much like you."

I blinked the tears from my eyes. It was the nicest compliment I had ever been paid. [109–111]

She stretcheth out her hand to the poor;
yea, she reacheth forth her hands to the needy.
PROVERBS 31:20

THE GIFT

White woman!"

Reluctantly I turned to face the village chief. He approached me, his face void of expression. I stood where I was, as custom demanded, with my eyes lowered. *Surely he will respect the lawman, even if he does blame the lawman's wife.*

"You do good," he declared loudly. "You save women and children—and wise old ones and our sick."

I shut my eyes and breathed a prayer of thanks.

"I give you best I have. I give you boy child."

I gasped. The very thing I wanted more than anything was being offered. I sent up a quick prayer. The minutes ticked by as I enjoyed the warmth of the baby in my arms. Then I took a deep breath, willed away my tears, and lifted my eyes.

"White woman has glad heart because of gift. Now I give chief a gift. I give you boy child." I passed the baby back to his father. "The debt is paid. You owe no more."

The chief signalled that the ceremony had ended.

"You shame us," LaMeche said softly. "You give—but not to get. From now on, it will take whole village to hold your friends. You will see." [121–125]

> *For God so loved the world,*
> *that he gave his only begotten Son.*
> JOHN 3:16

The chief pointed to the pot of simmering vegetables.

"What in pot?" he asked.

"Vegetables from my garden on the island."

He sniffed. Then stepped closer and sniffed again. "You grow there?"

"Yes."

"I am told island did not burn."

"It did not."

The chief studied me more closely, his dark eyes sending messages I did not understand.

"You make strong medicine to make food grow on cursed island and to make fire turn and run." And then he was gone.

I turned to Silver Star, who was stirring the cooking pot. She explained. "Chief says you have great power to make food to grow where evil curse had been. When one makes good to come from evil, then one has more power than evil."

"But I have no powers. None."

"Then why plants grow? Why Great One lead you from fire? Why you have wisdom to know what to do?"

I was confused and ashamed. How could these people be so—so superstitious as to believe I was some—some sorceress or something?

[132–133]

In all things ye are too superstitious. . . .
God . . . made the world . . . in him we live, and move.
ACTS 17:22–28

WORK

I come to Chief Crow Calls Loud to speak of garden. I know my garden is planted on island where none dared to go because of evil spell. I have no power over such evil. I know little about Indians' spells, and I am not strong against them. But I know Great God of all heaven and earth—same God who made all things and rules over all people. He is One who gives knowledge and power. In His name I come to Chief. People in need because of fire. We need much food. We need skilled braves to hunt. We need many hands to gather pine boughs to build shelters. We must all work together to care for village."

"What does Golden-Haired Woman want from chief?"

"Someone to tell people what must be done."

"You tell."

"No longer. Chief is back. Not fitting for woman to still give orders."

He nodded. "You tell me. I give orders."

In a few minutes the whole scene had changed. Everyone was busy with some assigned task.

"You must have magic powers to get the chief to dance to your drum," LaMeche teased.

His humor was what I needed to forget the heavy burdens.

"You not laugh when you hear what I give you to do," I teased back. [134–138]

Every man should . . . enjoy the good of all his labour.
ECCLESIASTES 3:13

DIFFERENT

I was returning to my own campfire when I heard a commotion. Across the distance I recognized Wynn. With a joyous cry I raced toward him.

"Elizabeth!" he exclaimed as he threw his arms around me. "Thank God you're safe. I was so frightened when I saw the village."

I stifled my sobs and tried to speak. "I'm so glad you are back. I missed you so much. There was no one to take charge."

Wynn looked at the family firepits, the shelters, the meat hung in trees, the fishnet that was taking shape, the new baskets.

"It looks very well organized to me."

"I'll tell you all about it after supper," I promised.

But it was LaMeche who explained to Wynn—in great detail—all the circumstances of the fire. I blushed with embarrassment. Wynn's eyes were big with wonder. Hearing it from LaMeche, I found it hard to believe myself.

As we walked to our shelter later that evening, Wynn asked what had happened to LaMeche. "He's different. Remember how you used to dread talking to him because he was so sullen?"

"He *is* different. I don't know what we would have done without him. He's been so much help. I guess the fire did it." I thought for a moment, then added, "I guess the fire changed a lot of things." [139–146]

We . . . are changed . . . by the Spirit of the Lord.
2 CORINTHIANS 3:18

PROMISE

The village was a sorry sight. Bits and pieces of logs stood where homes had been. Here and there an iron object raised its head through the debris, defying even the fire. I wanted to shut my eyes to it, but I couldn't. I studied it carefully as we walked along, trying to picture where everything had been.

"Look here," Wynn said when we reached the place our cabin had been.

My eyes followed Wynn's pointing finger. There in front of us stood my "promise" barrel, overflowing with rainwater. I could not believe my eyes. Here and there the protruding rags showed where we had worked on it. The tar discolored much of the outside, but it was holding water.

Tears sprang to my eyes, and I could not speak. I felt Wynn's arm slip around me and draw me close. I looked at him with wet eyes and noticed that his eyes were glistening, too.

"Oh, Wynn," I finally managed, "He kept His promise. Right in the middle of the fire."

"He always keeps His promises, Elizabeth," Wynn reminded me.

I looked at the remains of the village. "But it is so different than the way I expected."   [147–148]

O Lord God. . . . Thou hast kept . . .
that which thou hast promised.
2 CHRONICLES 6:14–15

CONVERSION

W ynn received word from headquarters that we were being transferred for the winter to Athabasca Landing, a larger settlement.

"What will we do in Athabasca Landing?" I asked Wynn.

"I will work in the office, supervising the two men who patrol the area. And I guess you can just be a lady of leisure."

I did not like the thought of having nothing to do but make beds and cook meals. It would be as bad as the last winter when I had nothing to do and nowhere to go. But I knew Wynn needed my support so I tried to sound somewhat enthusiastic.

"Guess we can stand it for a few months," I said.

Wynn pulled me close, then left to tell LaMeche the news.

When he returned, he was eager to talk. "After LaMeche and I discussed business, he asked me about you. He wanted to know how you had the inner strength and wisdom to save the village. I explained to him about our faith in Jesus Christ. Then he said, 'I wish I had a faith like that.' I told him that he *could* have faith like that. I told him that Jesus had died for him—that he could repent, receive the Lord Jesus as Savior, and be born into God's family. And he did, Elizabeth. We prayed together in the woods, and he is now a Christian!" [160–166]

Paul and Barnabas . . . declaring the conversion of the Gentiles . . .caused great joy unto all the brethren.
ACTS 15:2–3

MOVING

The driver shouted a command to the horses, and the slow wheels started to grind forward. We were on our way. I dared not look back. The tears fell freely down my cheeks. I did not want to see the strange little campsite beside the lake. I did not want to look at the villagers who were now my friends—including one who was now part of our spiritual family. I did not want to see the small island where my garden, now almost bare, had provided many meals for our fellow survivors. Nor did I want to see the charred remains of what once had been the village.

I forced myself to look ahead, to gaze at the winding trail that would lead us over the next hill, and many more hills before we reached the small settlement of Athabasca Landing.

What awaits us there? I wondered. Surely it could not be better than what we left behind.

Then I brought my thoughts under control. Did not the same God still have His hand upon me for good? In my sorrow over having to leave friends, had I forgotten that He was still traveling with me? I wiped the tears. Surely, if He had something better than all of this for me, it must be good indeed. [173–174]

When thou passest through the waters, I will be with thee . . .
thou wast precious in my sight . . . I have loved thee. . . .
Fear not.
ISAIAH 43:2–5

THINGS

Athabasca Landing was a small settlement, but to my delight it looked quite civilized. There were shops and places of business, and even some small churches and a school! I might enjoy my winter here after all. Our new home was made of lumber and painted white. It was not a grand place by any means, but coming from the small cabin of our last winter, we thought it looked more than comfortable. A neat little picket fence surrounded the property and near the door was a well with a pump. I thought of my trips to the stream with my bucket and marveled at the comforts of the modern world.

After exploring our new surroundings, Wynn and the driver began to unload our wagon. We had very little to unload. We did have the things we had decided were unnecessary for survival when we moved into the tiny cabin at Smoke Lake. In the crates were some of my most treasured possessions, and I was thankful to God they had been preserved for me. If it had not been for their being crated and stored on the wagon, I would no longer have them.

With the few things I had managed to grab before the fire, we had precious little. *But "things" don't seem nearly as important since the fire,* I thought as I looked at Wynn.   [176–177]

I count all things but loss
for the excellency of the knowledge of Christ.
PHILIPPIANS 3:8

184

WORSHIP

About thirty-five people gathered for worship on Sunday. Most were elderly women and women with young children. *Rather a morose and quiet lot,* I thought as I looked around.

The parson's sermon was about choices. "Ye cannot love God and mammon," he reminded us. "A choice has to be made." He expounded on the theme for fifty-five minutes, citing several examples—all from the "mammon" side of the issue.

I knew the preacher spoke with conviction. I knew it was a lesson every Christian must learn and practice. But my heart felt a little heavy as I walked down the steps of the church that first day back to worship after so many years of worshiping alone in the wilderness. I had so hoped for a note of joy. I wanted to praise. I wanted to worship. I wanted to fellowship. I felt I had not been allowed to do any of those things.

When we reached the gate of our home Wynn paused a moment, then asked, "After we have our dinner, would you mind if we went out alone somewhere for our own little praise service? Guess we've done it for such a long time I have the feeling that the day won't be complete unless we do."

I wanted to hug him. I did so need to worship.   [179–180]

*I beheld the voice of many. . . . Saying, . . . Worthy is
the Lamb . . . and [they] fell down and worshipped
him that liveth for ever and ever.*
REVELATION 5:11–14

SERVICE

The pastor called on us to welcome us to his church and to invite us to become an active part of the fellowship.

"What might we do to help?" asked Wynn.

The pastor's eyes showed surprise at Wynn's offer. He mentioned the need for Sunday school teachers and for someone to handle the music. We both volunteered to teach, and Wynn offered to lead the singing if I would play the piano.

"Would you?" the pastor asked sincerely.

"I would be happy to," I assured him.

He blew his nose rather loudly, put his handkerchief away, and fumbled for words. "You folks can't appreciate what this means to me—and to Martha. We sort of struggled along here—and it's been tough going. We served in larger parishes before, but we felt the Lord wanted us to give some of our years of service to a mission. I . . . think perhaps we did it backward. We should have spent our years in a mission first.

"Anyway, it has been hard for us. Especially for Martha. Wait until she hears the news. We've been praying for some time now—" He stopped and cleared his throat. Then he looked up with glistening eyes. "Well," he said, "one should not be so surprised when God answers. Just thankful. Just thankful."

[185–187]

If any man serve me, him will my Father honour.
JOHN 12:26

ABANDONED

Wynn and I were home reading one evening when there was a knock on our door. Wynn opened it, and there stood Henry, one of his Sunday school students, shivering in the cold night air. Wynn hurried him in and I found him something to eat. We asked no questions, but after Henry had eaten, he picked up his thin coat, mumbled his thanks, and headed for our door.

"Where are you going?" Wynn asked. "I understand your family has left town. Where are you staying?"

"I was gonna stay in the house, but today some guys came an' boarded it all up, an' I can't get in."

"So you have no place?"

"I'll make out," he said, suddenly taking on a tough stance.

Wynn looked at me across the head of the young boy, and I nodded in agreement. "Tell you what," Wynn said, "we have an extra bedroom. Why don't you just stay here? Of course, we'd expect you to work for your board. You'd need to carry wood and haul water. We'd also expect you to go to school every day. In return, you'd get your clothes and your meals. Is it a deal?"

Henry shuffled his feet. I had the feeling he was trying hard to keep a smile from appearing. "Guess so," he answered. The grin finally came to Henry's face in spite of his reluctance.

[212–213]

Pure religion . . . is. . . .
To visit the fatherless . . . in their affliction.
JAMES 1:27

DISTRESS

The calendar was quickly using up the winter months, and I looked forward to spring with mixed emotions. It could mean we would be returning to the village. I longed to go. I missed our Indian friends. I had been praying daily that God would somehow open the door so we could return and share the good news of Christ's coming to earth to live and die for mankind.

And yet when I thought about going back to the Indian people, I also thought of my Sunday school class. They, too, needed to know about Christ and His love. If we went, would there be anyone to teach them? But more than all that, I thought about Henry, our little deserted waif. Who would care for Henry? I tried to leave it all with the Lord. "Cast your burden upon the Lord," the Scripture said, and I cast it—and then I pulled it back—and then I cast it again. Then one day in my quiet prayer time I became totally honest before God.

"Lord," I said, "I am sick of worrying about Henry. I know that I am not the only person that You can minister through. I give Henry over to You, Lord. If You ask us to leave him with someone else, then I am going to trust that You will meet his needs and care for him—physically and spiritually. Help me to truly release him to You, knowing that You love and care for him. And help me not to take this burden of Henry's care back on my own shoulders again. Amen." [216–218]

We were comforted . . . in all . . . distress.
1 THESSALONIANS 3:7

ANSWERED PRAYER

Henry was out of breath, and his cheeks were flushed with excitement when he burst into the house. "Sergeant says to tell you that we'll be having a guest for supper," he said, gasping for breath. "A real live Indian. I saw him myself."

My excitement matched Henry's. I could hardly wait to find out which of our friends was visiting.

Our guest was a stranger. Wynn introduced him as Pastor Walking Horse. At dinner he explained how he had come to know the God of the Bible and had cast aside all of the superstitions of his forefathers. Now he wanted to teach his people. He had gone out to take training and was ready to go back with the truth. The chief of his own village had forbidden his return, so he was starting his work in Smoke Lake.

"They are wonderful people, and they are ready. We have been praying for someone to go to them. You are the answer to our prayers."

Two days later Wynn came home with his new orders. We would be staying in Athabasca Landing. This came as a surprise to both of us, though it shouldn't have. I had committed Henry to the Lord because I thought He would need me to care for the Indians. God had answered by sending a qualified young minister to the Indians and leaving Henry with me. I smiled. *One should never try to outguess the Lord.* [219–221]

I will call upon thee: for thou wilt answer me.
PSALM 86:7

INDEX